IT'S TIME TO RETHINK *Your* FASHION

Creating a Better Future

LALITA LOWE

'Curious and intrigued about all things textile from the craftmanship to the styling and a great color sense, Lalita's perception of fashion is global: it encompasses great looks, unique craftmanship and the impact of creative design in the world. It takes Lalita's special vision not to leave any of those out.'

Philippe David, Textile Design, Paris

'There is only one person I have the pleasure to know with such a clear and conscious outlook around fashion investment. Quality and versatility in clothes and accessories – always respecting trends but with a long-term vision – are imperative for Lalita Lowe.'

Evelyn Tye, Achtung Mode

'Her love and passion for sustainable Australian made fashion was instantly obvious. My observation of Lalita is her overwhelming love for the process of design to creation.'

Cindy Newstead, Professional Styling Academy

'Lalita has an innate sense of style with an extraordinary eye for detail. The fashion industry rightly is often criticised for prioritising consumerism and superficiality above all else. This is not the case with Lalita, who effortlessly combines style, ethics and substance.'

Kate Challis, Kate Challis Interiors

'Lalita, meeting you was such a refreshing experience. It is not often one is able to experience a young woman as creative and curious as you are. Having an endless drive for fashion and the arts. Your zest for color, all art forms and historical periods is rare. This does show in your work and your personal sketches. Also, your personal honesty and integrity speaks volumes. May your success continue.'

Joan White, Director, Paris Fashion Institute

'Your gentle encouragement and beautiful, non-judgemental nature gave me an extra little spring in my step and a new confidence to be me. Thanks again.'
Dr Sarah Bishop

'As a fashion educator I am thrilled to follow Lalita's passion to review and examine the alternatives to her fashion practice. Her perspective is encouraging, and challenging us to look towards the sustainable future of our fashion industry.'
Tina Marino, RMIT School of Fashion

ABOUT THE AUTHOR

Lalita Lowe is a personal fashion curator who lives in Melbourne Australia. She has a unique and global perspective on fashion. Having travelled the globe and lived in cities as diverse as Mumbai to Paris, she has truly seen the role that fashion plays in culture and identity and the way it connects people through its craft.

Fashion has been a part of Lalita's life from the outset, being surrounded by sewing projects and handmade techniques like spinning and weaving as a child. This started a lifelong fascination with fabrics and texture, and instilled in Lalita that fashion and clothing is always connected to a process – from the farm and the sheep that produced the wool all the way to the beautiful sweater it created.

In her early 20s Lalita took an unconventional leap and moved to India to study meditation and eastern traditions. It was a pivotal four years and truly changed her outlook forever. A deeply rewarding time personally, it also provided endless inspiration. From the incredible colours, silks and fabrics of India to the artisanal techniques of such a rich culture, it ignited a desire to work in the fashion industry.

Lalita has since researched and studied fashion around the world. She spent three years in Paris, where she worked with luxury designers and other industry leaders. Lalita has also worked in fashion in New York, studied the business of fashion as well as design in Paris, and studied design at one of the leading fashion institutions in Australia. Being invited onto the fashion advisory board of RMIT University after completing her degree was truly an honour and a joy to play a role for young designers of the future. Along the way she also picked up a degree in marketing. She is also a certified fashion stylist.

In recent years Lalita has become aware of the immense changes taking place in the industry. She has seen the impact the industry is having on the environment and how the lives of the people who work to make our clothes are compromised. She has also noticed a shift in the way clothing is valued. This prompted her to write this book to help people who follow and enjoy fashion to rethink their wardrobes so that they can look better while also feeling good morally and socially at the same time. Lalita is passionate about the artistry of fashion and is committed to seeing a return of value to the entire process of creation, as well as the way we view clothing overall.

Lalita enjoys anything that is small, like a petite handbag, or her daily intake of two squares of dark chocolate. She is also an avid meditator and enjoys waking up before sunrise each day for this much loved quiet time. When she's not working, she loves to spend time with her very cute and cheeky dog, Leo. They exercise in the parks of Melbourne; no gyms for them. Lalita is also famous (or infamous) for baking amazing profiteroles. Having spent so much time in France, it serves as a constant reminder of the wonderful city of Paris. And her friends say that her dark chocolate profiteroles filled with cointreau custard are perfect for breakfast, lunch and dinner (and a 2am snack).

ACKNOWLEDGMENTS

There are guides and special souls who come into our lives at the perfect moment and I have been fortunate to have so many of them. This book is the result of grace. Of personal discovery and reflection, of genuine effort, creativity and the hearts and wisdom of many.

Thanks to my mother for your love, support and enthusiasm; book writing wouldn't have happened without you. Thank you Andrew; every moment is full of love, not to mention laughter, beautiful walks and weekends. Jim Walker, thank you for everything, and you know what I mean. Joan White, creativity flourishes and doors open because of you. Merci beaucoup Evelyn Tye, friendship and fashion always (and maybe a few taxi detours on the way to Rue D'antin). Tracey-Lee Hayes, you understood my vision for the cover image and took it to a whole new level; thank you, even on one leg. Maria Gullace, impeccable make up, lots of laughs and a song recommendation. Thank you Michael Hanrahan and Anna Clemann from Publish Central; the care and attention you took with publishing this book was impeccable and first class (oh, and of course Archie and Lik supporting from the sidelines).

Sharon Wauchob, Josh Neville, Yoichi Horie, so much appreciation. Thanks Marni Fechter for an introduction and Malan Breton for the opportunity. Dawn Wolf thanks for two weeks in the midst of fashion week. Ma cherie, Elli Ioannou, off the plane and onto the runway, a Paris adventure, love and thank you. Philip Fimmano, thanks for the speedy statistic, and to both you and Li Edelkoort for continued inspiration on all things considered and creative. Christina Bomba, our knitwear conversation was much appreciated and time at your beautiful boutique an inspiration. Kate Challis, Cindy Newstead, Tina Marino, Philippe David, Sarah Bishop; thank you for your beautiful testimonials. Thank you Sammy and Malva Bottari, for further inspiring my knowledge and love for quality and the European aesthetic. Brett Lillie, our weekly phone calls kept me inspired and on track. Jayden, a quick message and you were onto it pronto, thank you. Vanessa and Paul, Suni, Pavani, Grace, Beta, Melissa Obeid, *gros bisous*. Thanks Leo Lion Lowe for being as bossy as ever and the cutest companion to boot. To the beloved, eternal gratitude and service.

First published in 2020 by Lalita Lowe

A catalogue entry for this book is available from the National Library of Australia.

ISBN: 978-1-922391-58-2

Printed in Australia by McPherson's Printing Group
Project management and text design by Publish Central, www.publishcentral.com.au
Cover design by Peter Reardon, www.pipelinedesign.com.au
Cover photograph by Tracey Lee Hayes, www.traceyleehayes.com

The paper this book is printed on is certified as environmentally friendly.

Disclaimer: The material in this publication is of the nature of general comment only,
and does not represent professional advice. It is not intended to provide specific guidance
for particular circumstances and it should not be relied on as the basis for any decision
to take action or not take action on any matter which it covers. Readers should obtain
professional advice where appropriate, before making any such decision. To the maximum
extent permitted by law, the author and publisher disclaim all responsibility and liability to
any person, arising directly or indirectly from any person taking or not taking action based
on the information in this publication.

Contents

'I think it is an opportunity
for all of us to look at our
industry and look at our lives
and rethink our values, and to
really think about the waste
and amount of money and
consumption and excess, and
I obviously include myself in
this, that we've all indulged in
and we really need to rethink
what this industry stands for.'

—Anna Wintour

Let's start at the beginning

As a fashion professional, I spend a lot of time talking to people about their views, their thoughts and beliefs around the state of the fashion industry and fashion overall, and I've found many people are asking the same questions as me. These questions are both small and personal and giant and global. They include:

- Which brands are doing the right thing and which brands should I buy from?

- How do I know if the manufacturing process for clothes I buy is ethical?

- What damage are the clothes I'm buying doing to the environment?

- Why do I buy clothes and never wear them?

- How many clothes do I really need?

- How much do I really know about the clothes I'm buying?

- What happens to my clothes when I no longer want them?

These are questions people the world over have been asking more and more these days. There is no doubt there's a lot of clothing on the planet, and that none of us want more clothes than we need or want to waste our money. At the same time, we want to keep our wardrobes new and relevant. How do we do that without being wasteful? We don't want to throw clothing away mindlessly, adding to landfill. We want to be satisfied with our fashion and love everything in our wardrobes. We want to feel good about what we own, as well as feeling good morally and ethically.

So, what is the path forward?

Over the last 10 years, I've changed a lot when it comes to fashion, what I buy, how I think about my clothes, my understanding of the industry, the good, the not so good and where it's all heading. What I've thought about the most is my role in all of this, and my own need to really rethink my fashion, in every way.

We are at a point in time when the tide on fashion is changing. An estimated US$500 billion in value is lost every year due to clothing being barely worn and rarely recycled, according to the Ellen MacArthur Foundation, a charity dedicated to creating a new, regenerative and more responsible fashion economy. We can't continue to produce clothing at the same rate or draw from natural resources like this without inflicting massive damage in many ways. A vast majority of this clothing is ending up as waste, creating many environmental problems. There's also the ethical issues related to unfair and inhumane working conditions. Many fashion brands are turning a blind eye to the people making their clothes, all the while allowing them to suffer. Wages fail to meet the daily needs of these garment workers, and work conditions stretch the definition of humanity.

Thankfully, the world is waking up. Well, we have to wake up because finite natural resources are being depleted and the earth is suffering because of it. Not only is it affecting the planet but it is also putting a big question mark over the future of younger generations.

Slowly, a movement has started, demanding change in the fashion industry. Brands are being called to transform their practices so any clothes they produce have either minimal impact or no impact on the environment. It's a big call, but it must happen now. There is no question that the fashion industry is one of the most resource-intensive industries on the planet. And this is why it's so important that fashion's entire existence is rethought and reset.

How is this going to happen? Fashion is also one of the most power-ful and influential industries around, and this means we can't just wait for it to change. We are the ones who buy or don't buy. We are the ones with the money in our pockets. The question is, who are we going to put our money behind, if at all?

We can each have much more influence on the world of fashion than we realise. Rather than looking far afield, it's time to start locally, and the closest place is in our wardrobes. It all begins with how we relate to clothing and what our values are. You would be surprised by just how much your choices make a difference in changing a culture. It comes back to our own personal fashion choices. It comes back to our own lifestyle. We must elevate our awareness and approach fashion with a completely new mindset.

You may be wondering how your actions would make a difference when you're just one person and there is so much damage and so much waste as a result of the fashion industry. We can't afford to take this position. We need to see ourselves as part of the driver for change. Remember the ripple effect of a pebble in water? Our actions are like that pebble – even one less garment bought or one garment repaired rather than thrown out makes a great contribution to the overall picture. But when we buy without a purpose or reflection we are contributing to a disposable culture.

Personally I have seen all sides of the fashion industry over decades, from small local designers to global brands. I have discussed the impact of the disposable mindset with industry professionals and come to understand the bigger picture of our relationship with fashion. I started in fashion working in a boutique where I learnt about the importance of fit and the difference that a well-made garment could have on a woman's or man's self-confidence. I saw transformations happen for people in an instant when, after trying on many outfits that were so-so, we discovered those perfect pieces that suited them magnificently. It was like a light bulb moment, and I loved seeing the effect it had on the way people walked and held themselves.

Later I studied fashion in Paris and went on to work in the industry there. These years were inspiring, uplifting and hard work. They opened my eyes to what true quality and inspired design is when it comes to clothing, and I was also given insight into the business side the industry. One of the gems to come out of this time in Paris was that it reminded me of my own desire to create and make beautiful pieces, and with this knowledge I returned to education to study fashion design.

My first few days returning to study felt familiar and exciting. I remember feeling that it was exactly where I belonged, among fabrics and patterns and the company of creatives discussing a vision. An interesting thing happened as the course went on: on the one hand I was so happy to be creating, but on the other hand I was learning in detail about the current state of the fashion industry. My relationship to fashion began to change, and the information I was uncovering in my own research was unsettling me.

This is when I began to rethink my relationship with fashion. I realised that the state of fashion was completely different to when I first started to appreciate design in my 20s. Fashion had become a numbers game, and with the entrance of 'fast fashion' the whole industry had changed. I realised that even though the integrity and incredible creativity of fashion still existed, the value of fashion in the mainstream market had been lost. The worth of artisanal items, textile quality and integrity, and the construction of a garment had shifted, and people now valued the new, easy to buy and easy to dispose of.

I also discovered the vast environmental and humanitarian issues that were arising, and started to ask myself why the world needed another fashion brand. I understood that what we all need is less clothing but better clothing. That a change needed to take place.

Throughout this book, you and I are going to look at all aspects of the fashion industry. We are going to walk through the doors of our personal lives to explore what fashion means to each of us. We will talk about our beliefs and perceptions of fashion, taking a deep dive to understand how we approach it today and how we can engage with it in the future. We will look at our own relationship to fashion and explore the landscape of the industry. There are so many factors that have contributed to the current situation, and these same considerations are forcing it to stop and change. You and I will look at what needs to happen in the future, and how we can be a part of it.

FASHION AS A FORCE FOR GOOD

What if there was a new way of doing things that created a better future overall? One that provided greater satisfaction with our own clothing. What if fashion could be used as a force for good? This is what we will explore throughout this book. The one thing that precipitates change is knowledge and information. And this is what I aim to do, to give you a new way of looking at things. To provide the information that will cause you to ask greater questions about your own relationship to fashion and how you can engage with it in a more uplifting and responsible way. As you discover a new approach to your own fashion you may just find it takes on a whole new meaning.

This book has been written to promote reflection, to educate and also to inspire change. Each of us has our own unique relationship with fashion and so there may be particular chapters that jump out at you. Feel free to pick up the book and start reading at whatever point inspires you. There will be a reason for it I am sure. And this is my main wish: that whatever part of the book you are reading, you be fully present, engage with it, contemplate it, take it on board. I want you to make it personal. As personal as you can.

Fashion, after all, is very personal.

If you find something that is challenging, or calls you to question your own beliefs, don't just discard it. Make note of it and take it upon yourself to ask how it relates to you. In what ways are you considered with your clothing, and how might you be able to improve?

This book is not about pointing a finger. It's written because I understand just how important fashion is in our lives. I am part of the fashion industry, and am inspired everyday by the incredible creatives who produce beautiful work. I'm inspired by the beautiful fabrics and garments created by talented people. It's with this appreciation that I have written this book.

Imagine if every piece of clothing in your wardrobe had a sense of meaning and value, that it reminded you of a story of the people who made it and the value that your purchase brought to a community.

Just imagine if you truly loved everything that you owned. If there wasn't one hum-drum item in your wardrobe. And if instead you opened your wardrobe each day inspired with what you could create as well as being reminded of the diversity and culture it came from.

As you read this book I encourage you to engage fully. Take it upon yourself to be open minded and use each chapter as an opportunity to refine your own fashion experience. This book will call on you to elevate your awareness. Why not take the call and run with it?

We are at a point in time where fashion is not only a personal issue but a social and environmental one. We all have a relationship with fashion, and it's one that fluctuates with the demands of our lives. Come with me as we explore all that fashion is, and can be in the future. Let's rethink our fashion so that it is the greatest representation of who we are and is created out of the ultimate respect for the people who make our clothes and the planet on which they are made.

PART I

Setting the scene

'There is no beauty in
the finest cloth if it makes
hunger and unhappiness.'

—Mahatma Gandhi

THE BEST PLACE TO START as we begin to rethink our fashion is looking at the myriad factors that are calling us to re-evaluate what fashion represents in today's world. We need to begin by defining our own relationship to fashion by putting it under a microscope. We also need to gain a better picture of the entire landscape of fashion and how it impacts our personal lives, and the world at large. From there, standing at a greater viewpoint, we will be able to see the necessity for change.

CHAPTER 1

Our intricate relationship with fashion

'Beauty begins the moment you decide to be yourself.'
— Coco Chanel

Clothing is a part of all of our lives, from functional outfits to beautiful works of art which inspire us to wake up everyday and engage with fashion. What we wear shapes our attitudes towards ourselves and presents us to the world. Our clothing also influences how others perceive us. A well-pressed, crisp white shirt says something completely different to a wrinkled one that was pulled out of the drawer. An exotic artisanal piece bought on a trip overseas has a completely different meaning from a polyester item bought at a cheap department store.

Personal style empowers us and shares our message with the world. When our clothing is congruent with who we are, when it suits our lifestyle and has a purpose, we feel great also. Being happy and comfortable in our clothes depends on so many things. It really is an intricate and personal experience. One day it can be up and one day it can be down. How we feel in what we wear is greatly influenced by our self-perception. How much we value ourselves and our lives.

It's also very much caught up in our relationship to size and beauty. Unfortunately the factors that influence this are wide and varied, from outside circumstances to internal dialogue. We all know the power of media to make us feel less than attractive when we see models and ideal lifestyles pushed at us on every platform imaginable. Even when we know this is not realistic and think it doesn't affect us, it still influences what society expects and how we feel our appearance should be. The main thing it comes down to is how we truly feel about ourselves.

FASHION AND SELF-PERCEPTION

This search for self-acceptance is part of what led me to fashion. I know this struggle all too well, and have definitely had my issues with self-image, like so many people. For many years I had low self-esteem, and it's taken continual effort for me to discover my self-confidence. I'm still working on it, but acceptance and contentment are a much bigger part of my life now. As a child and teenager, fashion became a way for me to express myself, and improve how I felt about myself by wearing the right thing for the right group of people. It gave me an identity as a teenager. Later on as a young woman, I realised just how much an outfit could influence the way I feel and confidently present myself to the world.

Once I truly discovered fashion it took on a new life, and for a while I was convinced I needed to wear only the best. I loved my designers, and my wardrobe received a major upgrade. I didn't need to wear designer from head to toe in an obvious way, but I was more designer-focused than ever. What an exploration, until I found a middle ground where my personal style became a mixture of the old and the new, of well-known and less prominent designers. To me, quality is the underlying component of my wardrobe and directs my choices.

I wasn't always fashionable, and have had many fashion faux pas. It's not as if being in the fashion industry meant I got it right every time. It was all an exploration, and some of those outfits are better left unseen. But the thing that has been truly worthwhile is the self-discovery that has accompanied this journey. When I was less confident, I would try to cover up my body or would wear things that weren't well looked after. As I became more assured within myself, I naturally chose clothing that honoured who I am, made me look my best and didn't break the budget but was a worthwhile investment.

Sometimes we can get used to dressing a certain way; it can feel comfortable and easy, and yet doesn't always mean we are dressing our best. How we dress can be a reflection of our self-image. If we try to cover up or hide the bits we are not happy with, it's possible this can result in a shapeless or wrongly fitted garment that makes us feel worse than we did to begin with.

Have you noticed that the way you feel about yourself affects how you dress and vice versa? When we wear an outfit that fits us perfectly and suits our body shape it can transform the way we feel. All these things contribute to our style, our perception of the world and our place in it. Self-perception is everything; it influences all our actions and choices, and what we choose to wear is based on this.

EVERY GARMENT TELLS A STORY

Fashion is alluring, intriguing, powerful. Every garment we own has a story to tell. How we bought it, where and when. The events we attended in that outfit. The career we built. The party stage. The dating stage. Travel and adventure. Falling in love. Marriage and babies. Each garment represents days, years and decades of our lives.

Clothing is part of not only our story but the stories of others. Every fibre and stitch of our clothing holds the stories of the people who made each item. It also tells the story of those who grew the fibres and made the fabric, a story of the earth and nature. It's not a slogan on the front of a garment – it's an intricate combination of events.

What we wear is also influenced by our culture, and what is happening in society on a local and global scale. An example of this was with the designs of Christian Dior for his debut collection in Paris in 1947, two years after the bitter end of World War II. His new look challenged the practical and sensible clothing which preceded it, and appealed to women wanting to break free in the post-war era. Christian Dior's whimsical designs brought back sensuality, and they played a crucial part in the recreation of French culture after the war.

If you think of more recent times and remember what everyone wore during lockdown amongst the Covid-19 pandemic, we were all at home in our leisurewear, wanting to be comfortable and feel at ease. What will we all be wearing as the world returns to normal? Will we be like those people of the post-war era wanting to celebrate life and all things beautiful once again? I hope so.

SEEING THE WHOLE PICTURE

When we start to recognise our relationship with fashion, when we see the whole picture, we get to understand how clothing influences us and is a result of our lifestyle. I'm sure that all of us, whether we are fashionistas or not, want to feel good in our clothes. We want to look at each garment and feel, *yes, that's me and that's what I want to wear*. But this doesn't always happen. Some of us have an innate sense of style, of proportion, colour, and what works for us. And others are still working it out. We don't get style training at the beginning of our lives, unless we grew up in fashion or had super-stylish role models. It's not a subject at school.

For example, it's so important to understand the basics of proportion. This simple and sometimes underestimated principle is all about perception. It can turn someone of average height into looking like an amazon, it can add weight or take it off, and it can add personality and flair or strip things down to be completely understated and demure.

Knowing what works for our own body shape and personality is the key to personal style. When you understand this it becomes much easier to make fashion purchases you love. Knowing the shapes and styles of clothing that suit you ensures you will keep the clothing you wear. It is also your personal armour against the incessant marketing of fashion brands.

Each fashion brand has their specific muse or type of woman or man that they design for. As they are creating a fashion collection and do the fittings for each piece of clothing, they have in-house models to make sure that every garment is designed accordingly. This model is usually under weight and above average height. This means the clothing we see in stores is often designed for a small group of people in our society. And when we try this clothing on, we wonder why it doesn't fit or suit us, often deducing that there is something wrong with *us*.

Then there is the marketing of these clothes, which are usually shown on underweight models without bumps or curves. These images make it hard for us to translate those looks into our own reality. The way we see clothing on a model more often than not is not the way this clothing will fit us. This can leave us disheartened when we go into a store to try something on, only to find it doesn't suit us. And this is because the clothing is usually not suited for our body shape and height.

Knowing how to translate what we see on the model or mannequin to how we want to look can take some education. It takes trial and error to work out what really suits. This applies especially to women because we have a wider variety of clothing, shapes and colours to choose from, not to mention each woman being unique in their curves from top to bottom. Men usually have fewer problems with this because even though each is unique in terms of size and height, overall they are more rectangular in shape and have less variety of colours and styles to choose from than women – however skinny jeans on the wrong body shape will never suit a man no matter how hard he tries.

Shopping for clothes can be joyful, but it can also be frustrating and disappointing. Unfortunately, it's also way too easy to get caught up in feeling like we need a new dress or a new outfit to look good, to be happy or present well. Over recent years, some types of clothing have become so cheap that many people view them as disposable; if they don't like something they either send it back or dispose of it. Wearing an item once has become acceptable because its cheap price tag means it's easy to just get something new to suit the next moment and the next mood of the day.

This is where fashion has become really complicated over recent years. More and more clothing is being produced, worn only a few times and thrown away. It's a buy-and-dispose-of mentality that is creating a huge waste problem, which we will explore later. This culture has also devalued clothing, which is a true loss for what clothing should be: an expression of craft, skilful design and an endless array of mindfully created textiles.

FASHION AND GLOBALISATION

More than ever, we need to be conscious about what we buy and how, not only for our own sake but also for what that clothing implies. When we used to buy a garment it was often good quality. It was special if it came from overseas and held a unique look and style. But as the world has become more globalised and more readily accessible, this has started to lose its meaning. The world is also becoming more gentrified.

These days a lot of clothing is a reflection of our interconnected world, and the garments we buy are losing their unique cultural identity. They no longer signify a unique culture or location. Artisanal work has been pushed into the background. Borders around the world have blurred, and respect for the creation of clothing in relation to a local identity and culture has been lost in a world of mass production. This has created a multitude of social, ethical and environmental issues.

We are becoming more aware every day of the need to be conscious about how we consume on this planet. It's part of a growing consciousness that it's not the amount of things that matter but the quality. It's time to come back to a simplified existence that honours the effort, resources and time it takes to produce something of value. In this way, we express our respect for life on this planet and everything that makes up a rich and connected human experience. For this to happen, we need to rethink our fashion and make a conscious decision of how we want to engage with it.

CHAPTER 2

There's so much more involved

'If we don't work with our fellow creatures and with our
planet in mind, we will destroy the thing that keeps us alive.'
— Stella McCartney

Fashion has changed. The way people value it has changed. In recent years it's become very obvious that the way the industry operates has become unsustainable and has reached a tipping point. It's time to review not only our relationship with the clothes in our wardrobes but also the world of fashion as a whole.

A RAPIDLY GROWING PROBLEM

The fashion industry is one of the most resource-intensive industries in the world. It is a major contributor to the depletion of the world's natural resources, and many of its processes are harmful to our environment. Manufacturing is also putting the lives of the people who make our clothes at risk.

Each year it's becoming more and more obvious that we are vulnerable to our environment. We are dependent on the elements of nature being in balance. When irregular events happen like freak storms, the seasons becoming warmer, or massive schools of fish being washed up on a beach, it's clear that the balance is off.

Some people discount the escalation of unnatural weather patterns and say they are just a cycle of nature. Scientists, on the other hand, paint a different picture. They tell us our planet is in trouble, that nature is a delicate ecosystem which has been thrown out of order. They also tell us that natural resources are being used up and our environment is unable to regenerate as quickly as it is being depleted.

Some of the biggest contributors to this damage are large-scale farming, manufacturing, transportation and the overproduction of new materials. If you think about the clothes we wear and everything it takes to create them, it's no surprise to discover this involves all of these industrial processes. Globally, fashion is a trillion-dollar industry. It exists on such a huge scale that the environmental and humanitarian problems it has created are immense.

There is so much waste and pollution created that people, communities, cities and governments are waking up to the problems that have come as a result. When a fashion brand creates a collection of clothing, it starts a chain of events that consumes resources and creates waste. It even begins before the design process, right back to farming and the way textiles are produced. Conventional textile production involves many chemicals and is responsible for considerable global greenhouse gas emissions.

Within the design houses themselves there are massive amounts of resources used to take a collection from concept to creation. Outside the design room, pollution, waste and environmental damage is created right through the production process. And it doesn't stop there because the amount of clothing being produced is increasing globally year on year, and much of it is ending up as waste.

The textile waste of the fashion industry is beyond imagination; it's happening within production and extends long after an item has reached our wardrobe. Think of just one tiny part of the manufacturing process, like when fabric is cut from a pattern. Each time a roll of fabric is used, textile waste is created. When a pattern is placed onto fabric it's arranged like a set of jigsaw pieces and then cut out, and what is left over is the fabric remnants. Now think about how many millions of pieces of clothing are created annually. Producing this much clothing leads to massive quantities of fabric remnants which are left over as waste and need to be discarded.

There are also toxic chemicals that go hand in hand with the garment industry. These chemicals are used to dye our clothing. Chemicals are also used to treat the fabrics our clothes are made of. As natural and man-made fibres are turned into fabrics, toxic chemicals are brought into play. According to the Ellen MacArthur Foundation, the dyeing and treatment of textiles causes 20% of industrial water pollution globally. The chemical waste from these processes doesn't just evaporate into thin air. It stays around, creating a host of problems in waterways, soil, agriculture – not to mention our own wardrobes. Do you ever think about the chemicals that may be touching your skin when you put on that new sky-blue woollen sweater or stunning red silk dress?

CLOTHING WASTE

Our wardrobes are the site of a host of problems, including clothing waste. The average Australian buys approximately 27 kilograms of textiles per year. The startling part of this is that they dispose of about 23 kilograms of this clothing per year. Where do all these clothes go? According to the Ellen MacArthur Foundation, less than 1% of material used to produce clothing is recycled into new clothing, and this means that most of it ends up as waste. If it ends up in landfill it can take up to 200 years to decompose. Unfortunately, most of this clothing will never decompose because it's made of manmade fibres like polyester, a type of plastic made from petroleum which, once created, is almost impossible to break down.

Then there is the clothing waste created by the fashion industry. No one talks about what happens to all the stock that goes unsold in stores when a new season rolls around. This clothing has to go some-where when nobody wants to wear it, and more often than not it also ends up in landfill or is incinerated.

THE HUMAN IMPACT

Along with the environmental impact, there is also the personal, human-itarian impact. The hearts and lives of people are at risk. More often than not the clothing we buy is being sewn by people whose rights are taken advantage of. Working conditions are below what is considered ethical or safe. Garment workers are often abused and exposed to extreme conditions. Working conditions are compromised not only when our garments are sewn but also in farms and around the machinery, tanneries and chemical treatment rooms that make our clothing look pristine when we buy it instore.

The value of clothing has also changed. Clothing was once celebrated for its exquisite workmanship and design. Makers and artisans were respected for their ability to turn a piece of fabric into stunning shapes and forms. We looked for this kind of quality and were willing to pay for it. However, over time the value of a garment has diminished due to a rise in production and a decrease in cost. The average person is willing to pay less, and they place more importance on its relevance in the moment than its quality and longevity.

When we buy a garment, the cost should contribute to the entire line of production in a way that respects its value. It should honour a tradition and contribute to a particular skill or craft. In indigenous artisanal communities, thread and yarn are a symbol of many hours of work, and the handmade pieces that are created contribute to the wellbeing of an entire community. These items are made out of purpose and they represent a circle of tradition.

THE INDUSTRY MUST CHANGE AND SO MUST WE

Craftsmanship like that of Savile Row tailors was once revered and sought after. It still holds this value today, however the demand for garments of such quality has decreased. The designer Alexander McQueen trained and acquired many of his skills in Savile Row. He would not have been able to create the incredible pieces that he did without those essential design capabilities. And it's this kind of quality that is being overshadowed by the fast, cheap and disposable methods of the industry.

Clothing should be celebrated. It should be made and sold out of respect for the skill, effort and resources used to produce it. How do we sift through this web to find brands that truly value this process? How do we spot true value and know what to invest in? Shouldn't it be the fashion industry taking responsibility for their practices? If the fashion industry can have such a negative impact on people and the environment it also has the power to turn it around. At the same time, we are the ones who consume fashion. We are the ones who buy the clothes, and we can also have the power to influence change. We can drive this change by putting our money in the right direction and making the right fashion choices.

The industry must change and so must we. Overall, we are at a point in time where the role of fashion must return to a considered and wholistic state. My vision is that there is a return to true craftsmanship and a respect for the entire process of design. The fashion industry can no longer exist in a state of overproduction. It has a big part to play in averting an environmental disaster, and it is also responsible for returning prosperity and true welfare to all the people who offer their lives in service of our clothes.

CHAPTER 3

Can we stimulate positive and lasting change?

'Become an active citizen through your wardrobe.'
— Livia Firth

What does it take to facilitate true change? Whether it's personal, corporate or global, change and transformation only take place when something else becomes more important. We are at that point right now with fashion. There are too many warning signs to ignore. The old system has reached its use-by date and industry leaders have realised this. You and I also know that we need to be making more conscious decisions about what we buy and wear. This is what inspires me and shows me that we are heading in the right direction.

What is positive change in fashion? Positive change is putting the wellbeing of the environment and people first. The industry is at a tipping point. It has been unsustainable for many years now. There has been a lot of talk about the need for more sustainable and responsible business models, and now is the time to act. This doesn't mean just 'a little bit' sustainable. It's a complete reorientation of the way clothing is designed and produced.

This issue is extremely complex. There are so many people involved as well as huge numbers of livelihoods. From small farmers to the big-name fashion designers. Change requires every person and business in the fashion industry to move towards more efficient, environmentally friendly and human-centric ways of creating clothing. To create this type of lasting change, businesses and industries will need to collaborate and agree to work together on a more sustainable fashion system, some of which is happening today.

THE ONE THING WE CAN RELY ON

Yes, the future is uncertain; we don't know whether the industry is going to change as radically as it has to. We also don't know whether people will act quickly enough for it to have any immediate and positive effect on the environment. The one thing we *can* rely on is our own personal decisions. There is a lot that you and I can do, and we have so much more ability to be a positive influence than we may realise.

This book talks a lot about the state of fashion and the industry – my intention is that it offers greater insight so you can make better choices in your own life where they are needed. For positive and lasting change to take place we need to rethink our own relationship with fashion, how we dress, how we take care of our clothes, our values around fashion and who we buy from. We need to understand what the implications are before we hand our money over for that new black silk dress or blue woollen suit.

It's up to you how you spend your money.

Recently a woman reached out to me on social media to share her experiences with fashion. As a married mother in her 40s she told me that she has recently made the shift to a simpler and cleaner way of urban living. Because of this new lifestyle, she has found it hard to find clothing which aligns with this new and refined approach. She wants to find quality clothing to reflect her values. She wants to make purchases that also take care of people and the planet.

IT CAN BE CHALLENGING

It's inspiring to hear stories like this, and I find that it's becoming increasingly common for people to share how they are being more considered with their fashion. Hearing women and men talk about their newfound awareness gives me hope that the conversation of fashion's impact on the environment as well as the humanitarian cost is really is starting to take hold. It's encouraging and uplifting to think there is a return to value when it comes to the clothing people want to wear and buy.

My aim is that this book gives you enough knowledge to rethink your approach to fashion, as well as giving you enough tips to make positive personal choices. Approaching fashion in a considered way may require that you question some of your current beliefs. You may feel the desire to question some of the choices you have been making to this point. Making positive choices may require some fine tuning, or even a paradigm shift. I understand it can be challenging, and it's something I am also working on everyday. I am up for it, and have already been taking steps to reduce my impact on this beautiful planet. Each day I aim to be more conscious of my actions.

Will you come on board? I hope so.

CHAPTER 4

It's not going to be easy but it's going to be worth it

'A careful and intelligent slowdown is the only way out, a road that will finally bring value back to our work.'
— Giorgio Armani

Rethinking our fashion does takes some work. It requires us to ask questions, to evaluate our own relationship with fashion, and question the practices of the brands we usually buy from. It may be uncomfortable in the beginning because what you find may not always align with sustainable and ethical conditions. But if you do go down this road it's going to be worth it. It will lead to a more satisfying experience of fashion. It will also help to create a better future for the environment and the people involved in the production process.

YOUR PERSONAL STYLE

Fashion has become associated with buying and acquiring more and keeping our look new in the process. My viewpoint on fashion is different. I believe we don't need to keep buying more in order to develop a relevant and amazing collection of clothes. Personal style is very different to consumption.

When you get to a point where you don't need much in life to be content, that is a good place to be. That's not to say you don't like, want or have beautiful things in life. When you appreciate stylish and elegant things, including well-made clothes, you want your life to be filled with them. It's an outlook and a way of being. Having this kind of appreciation is a big part of enjoying life. Being content is more about being at peace in your life, and is enhanced when you are surrounded by the things that truly bring you joy.

So personal style is more about the types of clothes you have and how you wear them. Whether they are a true reflection of you. Personal style comes down to what we value, and when you decide you only want to have things in your life that hold value then it doesn't matter how little or how much you have. You can get satisfaction from one single outfit alone. Just putting it on and wearing it brings you joy because you have made a very conscious decision to have it in your life.

Just think of a precious item you currently own − it could be a piece of clothing or something else. A painting. A musical instrument. A piece of jewellery. Think of an item that has a story behind it. You know where it came from and how it was made. Perhaps you even met the artist or the designer. Do you know about the inspiration behind that piece? And how long have you had it? Maybe years? Maybe it's a family heirloom. And does it give you great satisfaction to know all these things?

Imagine if you loved the garments in your wardrobe just as much. Just picture all the pieces you own holding the same kind of meaning and value. You view them like an investment and they were carefully considered purchases. The way you handle and take care of them is out of respect for the people who made them and where they came from. Taking this approach also means that you are valuing yourself and your life in the process.

MANY OF THE PROCESSES INVOLVED IN MAKING OUR CLOTHES THESE DAYS ARE COMPROMISED

So, how does this relate to rethinking fashion on a bigger scale? When we value what we have in our life, it means we're willing to invest in it. But how can we invest in something when we learn that the conditions in which it was made are compromised? Many of the processes involved in making our clothes these days are compromised. This means we need to be asking questions and making better buying decisions. It's not always an easy process, because it means we need to do our homework and put some effort in.

Rethinking our fashion is really an exploration because it involves finding out about the things that really do create a well-made garment. A well-made garment is also one that is made out of respect. You take into account the quality of the fibre, the workmanship, the fabrics and the purity of the dyes. You also learn about the process and the people behind it. It's a wholistic approach. Imagine discovering a whole new world of fashion that you had never come across before.

Finding the right information will allow you to make conscious and considered decisions. Making better decisions can sometimes mean making an investment, and it can also mean spending nothing at all. It may take effort in the beginning, but that's what I'm here to help you with. You will learn to see beyond surface value like a good bargain or beautiful slogans that tout sustainability. You will learn how to look for brands that have environmental and humanitarian values at the core of what they do. This means you end up engaging with a story, you engage with the values of a brand and the process it took to make your garment. The next item you buy then has a whole lot more meaning and significance.

Rethinking your fashion will also challenge your thinking about how many clothes you really do need. It will ask you to examine any habits that treat clothing as disposable. It will require you to up your game in terms of taking care of what you own so that it lasts longer. This new approach will call on you to redirect the urge to buy a garment on a whim and instead ask, *what do I already have in my wardrobe that could suit this need? How can I reimagine and restyle the clothing I already have?*

This all takes a bit of work. I'm not saying it's going to be a breeze to take some time to ask fashion brands about their practices or to do some extra research to find out the story behind any clothing you may buy in the future, but I promise that it will be rewarding. Making better choices like this and digging deeper means you are doing your part to shift fashion in a positive direction.

Along with making better fashion choices, rethinking fashion will also inspire a specific approach to life, one that is truly mindful and compassionate. I'm sure you care about the future of the planet as much as I do. I'm also sure you want to know that the people who make your clothes are taken care of and not just treated like second-class citizens. Rethinking your fashion is about doing everything you can to make sure your wardrobe is a representation of that.

CHAPTER 5

How to use this book

We're about to get into the juicy parts of the book, so let me tell you a bit about how to use it. I want you to use *It's Time to Rethink Your Fashion* in a way that works for you. This book is many things — it's designed to educate, to prompt reflection, and also to inspire action. There are chapters that may challenge your thinking about fashion. They may inspire some contemplation and ask you to reflect on your own experience.

There will be other chapters that are practical and down to earth. Please take the time to engage fully, and if you can, allow the insights to percolate and take hold inside you. You may want to use a notebook to write down what comes up for you. You may also want to take some time to review your own fashion collection as you get further into the book — my advice is, *go for it*. If nothing else, a review and refinement of your approach to fashion so that you are more satisfied with what you have would be a great outcome.

This book is designed as a call to action. It's written to prompt you to move. To think about how you currently approach fashion and then review any insights or 'a-ha moments' and then make new choices.

Feel free to pick up the book at any chapter and read it. It could be the one that inspires you to love yourself more and to take care of everything with more attention. Just one chapter could inspire you to search out new fashion brands that align with you ethically and environmentally.

And now, let's get into it.

PART II

What does it mean to rethink?

'Fashion with a big F is no longer there. And maybe it's not a problem; maybe it's actually a good moment to rethink.'

—Lidewij Edelkoort, Trend Union

ANY TIME WE BECOME AWARE that we need to make a change in our lives, what do we do? We stop. We take stock and we review what we have been doing to date. Then we gather new information about ways to move forward. With the new knowledge, we can them make informed and inspired decisions that will lead to a greater experience.

Being prepared to review something takes a deliberate approach. It requires an open-hearted willingness. It also requires us to connect with our passion for whatever it is we are going to review. And it also requires us to look at something from all angles, and to be prepared to put our own personal agenda to one side. To keep it in consideration, and at the same time to be prepared for a transformation.

Fashion as a whole has always been about renewal and reinvention. Fashion has reflected cultural and social changes throughout the decades. It has created new genres and started cult-like followings. At some point in the last decade fashion started to lose its meaning. Why? Because the integrity of design and creation was taken off centre stage and replaced with super-fast lines of production.

To create a new model, we first need to stop. We need to review and understand the current situation, and we need to consciously choose how we are going to engage with fashion. It really does require that we rethink fashion in every way and design a new way forward.

CHAPTER 6

Most of us have a desire to be better

'Look good, feel good, and do good — that's as good as it gets.' — Rosario Dawson and Abrima Erwiah

We are at a point where we need to rethink everything about fashion. It's time to review what it means to us personally, because the statistics show that our relationship with fashion often leads to unworn garments, unsatisfying purchases and wasted resources.

Most of us feel that we can be better people, and I believe most of us *want* to be better. I'm not trying to say anyone is bad or not a good person at all, but I do think that there is a natural inclination within each of us to grow and be better. To do and feel better. To not damage, to not pollute and to not harm others.

Taking what we have covered so far into consideration — doesn't it prompt you to want to make a difference? When we recognise that inequality exists and that damage is being done to the environment, it does call on our own humanity and ask us to contribute. In terms of fashion, it does make us ask, 'How can I look good as well as feeling good both morally and environmentally?'

Why not allow this desire to grow so that you have no choice but to make decisions in alignment with your values and highest vision for yourself and the planet?

CHAPTER 7

Rethinking our wardrobes

'Style is the only thing you can't buy. It's not in a shopping bag, a label, or a price tag. It's something reflected from our soul to the outside world — an emotion.' — Alber Elbaz

There are two elements to rethinking our wardrobes. One is to do with looking and feeling great. The other is about our buying decisions and their impact on the planet and the people who make our clothes. Ideally we want to be better in both.

A new approach to fashion calls for action. Where does it start? Our own personal wardrobes. Rethinking what we wear and how we choose our clothes is liberating. In the coming chapters we will revisit, rekindle, redress, recondition, rearrange, rebuild and reimagine our fashion and our relationship with it.

FEELING AND LOOKING GOOD

Rethinking our wardrobes is about making sure we have the pieces that represent who we truly are. Gone are the days of buying things we don't need or that don't suit us because of a lack of purchasing thought. (Well, there may be a few mistakes, but that's human.) Later in the 'doing' section of the book you will learn how to craft an incredible collection of clothes. You will learn how to choose so that any new items you do buy are worth the investment and will serve you for a long time.

Rethinking our wardrobes is about crafting an approach to fashion based on quality and longevity. These are the things that will bring true satisfaction with any garment or outfit. Rethinking our fashion is a homage to great style and better buying decisions.

Rethinking our personal wardrobes involves the following:

- understanding how body shape, proportions and colour determine what looks good on you

- knowing how to find the right fit

- making sure your personal style represents who you are, and how you want to be and feel

- understanding how your clothes make you feel and why

- asking if your clothes suit you as best as they could

- knowing if your clothes are breathable and comfortable

- making sure your clothes suit your lifestyle

- checking whether your clothes are age relevant

- making sure your clothes represent you in the best way possible.

Many times we assess these things without realising we are doing it. On the other hand, if we consciously pay attention to our choices and understand why we make them then we have so much information to help us craft our wardrobes in the way we would like.

I'm not saying yours isn't already a great wardrobe or collection of pieces, or that you're not happy with it. But what I am saying is that many times we feel like it could do with some refinement. It's like recently when I realised that I wanted to feel more feminine in what I wore – I took a look at what I owned and I saw mostly pants and less feminine items. It was very obvious to me that I needed to own some skirts and softer pieces.

There are many things that get in the way of us having the style and clothes we would like. It can be because of limited time, shifting values, lifestyle, available resources and income, and of course the big one: body shape. The good news is that none of these mean you have to compromise on style or a truly amazing collection of pieces that make you feel your best.

Knowing how to dress for your body shape is one of the most important parts of personal style. It enables you to highlight your best features and camouflage other areas. Once you become familiar with the key shapes and proportions that make you look your best, it's so much easier to buy clothes you look and feel good in. This in turn means it's more likely you will keep them for longer.

Rethinking our wardrobes in terms of personal style means we need to be practical and understand our needs; only then do we have the tools to be creative and add some flair. All this goes a long way to making decisions that will serve us well into the future. It's about making fabulous decisions so that we reduce the number of 'what was I thinking' pieces that lead to clothing and financial waste. Which leads us into thinking about the environment and considering the people who make our clothes.

DOING THE LEAST AMOUNT OF HARM POSSIBLE

Rethinking our wardrobes also helps us to make choices that have a beneficial impact on the environment and contribute back to the people who make our clothes. To do this we need to consider:

- what our clothes are made of
- different fabrics and the chemicals that may or may not be used
- quality over quantity
- durability so clothes last and you will keep them longer
- clothes that are designed and made well so they will last
- the waste in our wardrobes and why we don't wear those items
- the price we paid for our clothes and whether it is appropriate for the garment
- how we can buy more consciously
- having a strategy so we don't buy things we won't wear
- realigning our choices with more ethical and environmental considerations.

Rethinking our wardrobes so that our clothing does the least amount of harm means knowing what goes into our clothes that makes them sustainable; it also means understanding the value of a garment and being prepared to buy pieces that have been made out of respect for nature and the people who make them.

It also means understanding how to buy clothing that will last. We also want to know what our clothes are made of because some fabrics have more environmental implications than others. Some fabrics are made with chemicals and some aren't. Some clothing is made of fabrics that release microfibres into the oceans, affecting waterways. We need to understand what each of these are.

Our clothing started somewhere as a fibre and ends up in your wardrobe. We need to consider what will happen to it afterwards. We don't want it to finally impact the environment as landfill. On the other hand, if we choose well, clothing can continue to provide pleasure for years to come in your collection, and the wardrobes of people after you, perhaps even your children or grandchildren. We have a choice.

It all comes back to the goal that we can have a wardrobe of beautiful clothes that make us feel and look our best while also doing as little harm as possible to the planet and the people on it.

CHAPTER 8

Rethinking fashion locally, nationally and globally

'If you're trying to create a more just and a more
sustainable world, fashion is a good place to start.'
— Paul Van Zyl

Rethinking our wardrobes is now a bigger issue than the types of clothes we like to wear. It's a social issue, and an environmental one. Not all clothes are created equal: some have a bigger impact on the environment than others. Some are made in unethical conditions. But how are we to know if we don't have the information, or if we don't socialise in fashion circles where people talk about these issues often?

We need to be aware of what we are buying so that our clothes are almost like a vote. A vote for the health, wellbeing and future of our planet. A humanitarian vote for the hearts and rights of the people who make them.

Fashion used to be much more considered. The clothes we wore had meaning; we were surprised and delighted by new styles and shapes coming out. Adventurous design was celebrated for its ability to break through to a new silhouette. It was a way to keep us engaged with culture. We thought more about the pieces we bought because generally they cost more, which meant we had less clothing and valued it more.

THE PROBLEMS CAUSED BY 'FAST FASHION'

A lot of this has been forgotten. On the whole, we have way more clothes on the planet and in our wardrobes than we need. For the average customer, most of this clothing has been created by 'fast fashion'. Fast fashion relates to trend-based clothing that is produced quickly and in huge quantities for very little cost. It makes the most stylish outfits available to all, but unfortunately this clothing is made poorly from inferior fabrics.

The claim of one of the biggest fast-fashion companies is 'from runway to store in two weeks', which means that they replicate and interpret trending styles from the runway and get them made as soon as possible. This is a ridiculous model, and the crazy thing is that they achieve it. This clothing is pumped out just like the production line in a cookie factory. But this clothing is not made with the same quality of its twin from a designer runway.

The $80 suit jacket and $10 t-shirt in fast fashion is made of cheap, inferior fabrics with minimal care for how it is constructed, and this means it is often not made to last. There is even a term in fast fashion for an item designed to be worn once: 'never washed and thrown out'.

Fast fashion designs and creates clothing to an unreasonable timeline. In the traditional model it takes approximately nine months to prepare a collection from design all the way to delivery instore. It takes time to create a well-thought-out collection, designs that fit well and are made well. When I worked in Paris I saw this first hand. There were many hours spent on the fit of the garment, let alone the sourcing of fabrics and creation of the patterns.

With fast fashion, the only way they can produce hundreds of thousands of garments in short timeframes is to lower the time and cost of production and materials. They compromise on quality and squeeze manufacturers for tight timeframes, which then has an impact on garment workers. More often than not, machinists and garment workers are paid less than a living wage. These people are timed on the production of each piece of clothing, with unrealistic expectations and conditions far below what is acceptable in anyone's definition of normal. It's a major humanitarian problem.

This cheap, trend-based clothing has disrupted the entire fashion system. Fast fashion has devalued clothing. The average consumer now expects to pay less. Fast fashion has become the new normal for many people, and it has created a ripple effect throughout the rest of the industry. Because people now expect new styles more often, it has forced the luxury houses to try to compete, and so over time they too have tightened their schedules.

The issue is that for truly well-made, well-designed clothing to be produced it has to be done at a realistic and considered pace. It takes time to get a design fitting perfectly. But luxury houses started adding in extra collections to their schedules. On top of spring/summer and autumn/winter collections we then had resort and 'pre-fall collections'.

Many designers have started to push back. They have shared how unrealistic this schedule actually is. It squeezes a designer's creativity, creates huge amounts of stress and puts enormous pressure on production teams. Giorgio Armani recently commented on this in an open letter to *WWD* magazine. He said:

> The decline of the fashion system as we know it began when the luxury segment adopted the operating methods of fast fashion, mimicking the latter's endless delivery cycle in the hope of selling more, yet forgetting that luxury takes time, to be achieved and to be appreciated. Luxury cannot and must not be fast. It makes no sense for one of my jackets or suits to live in the shop for three weeks before becoming obsolete, replaced by new goods that are not too different.

So as you can see fast fashion has affected the entire industry. It has changed people's perception of what a garment is worth, and until recently there was no education about the impact of this clothing on the environment.

Another issue is the amount of clothing being produced. People are buying more, wearing it less and then sending it to the trash. Most of it is made of polyester, a type of plastic made from petroleum. When it's thrown out, it's usually sent to landfill where it will never decompose.

The environmental implications are huge. Not to mention the toxins that are used in the production process. Polyester clothing also has ramifications for our waterways: when washed, it releases tiny microfibres which eventually get washed into our oceans and this means they end up in our food supply.

The issue of microfibres ending up in the oceans is just a part of the huge environmental impact the production of clothing is having on the environment. But this environmental damage was occurring way before fast fashion; it's just that now it has been amplified. There is a huge drain on the earth's resources within the fashion industry. There are also vast amounts of waste and pollution created day after day across the world. We will go into all of these issues in more depth later.

The pace of fast fashion doesn't seem to be slowing down anytime soon, however in 2013 a significant event took place which exposed the true nature of production. It exposed systemic issues that could no longer be ignored.

THE RANA PLAZA FACTORY COLLAPSE

On Tuesday 23 April 2013, a large factory in Bangladesh India, called Rana Plaza, had been warned that there were cracks in the walls and they should close immediately. They were advised not to open the factory the following day, but this advice was ignored. On Wednesday 24 April, not long after staff had entered the building and begun work, the entire factory collapsed. It was a devastating – and significant – moment in fashion. More than 1100 people were killed. It was a tragedy. Families lost their loved ones, and anyone who did manage to survive the event was scarred forever.

This horrible event brought to light the long-standing issues behind fast fashion and the problems it was creating. Before Rana Plaza collapsed, fashion was a closed book. No-one would share where their clothing was being made or the suppliers they sourced their materials from. When that building came down and answers were sought, it was brought to light that many fashion brands were putting huge pressure on manufacturers.

They were demanding their extremely large quantities of clothing be made in shorter and shorter timeframes for cheaper prices. The bosses in these factories then passed on this pressure to the women and men making the garments. They were given unrealistic targets and were punished if they didn't reach them.

All of the issues that arise from fast fashion started to be exposed following this event. There has been a lot of investigation, and it has opened up a wider conversation about the conditions the fashion industry exists under. The amount of attention that unfolded has called for fashion brands to be more transparent about how their clothes are made and where their fabrics, trims and other resources come from. It has started a movement.

While a lot of action was generated after Rana Plaza, it appears we are still a long way from a responsible and ethical fashion industry. Many brands continue to sweep things under the carpet, choosing profit over the environment and people. To those of us in the fashion industry these issues are well known, but the public awareness is low.

There is a growing number of millennials who are consciously seeking out information and pushing for a more transparent, sustainable and ethical industry. They are choosing to buy less and to buy clothing produced sustainably and ethically. They are leading the charge for greater awareness about the industry. Overall though, the lack of awareness about the implications that a single purchase can have is widespread. This means there is so much education that needs to take place.

CHAPTER 9

It's time to act consciously

'Don't be into trends. Don't make fashion own you, but you decide what you are, what you want to express by the way you dress and the way you live.' — Gianni Versace

There are many times in life when we act out of habit and then realise later that we could have made a different choice. It's only on reflection after the experience or from seeing the impact of our actions that we become aware we need to do things another way.

Fashion is not something we think of as having too much consequence. Often when we buy pieces that don't suit us, it's not much of an issue and we just send it back or exchange it. Or we never wear it, and it sits at the bottom of our closet and we go on with our lives. But these decisions are important and they do have an impact. Little things matter, and they add up over time.

A SINGLE WHITE COTTON T-SHIRT

Individually it may seem like one white cotton t-shirt for $10 is a good buy. We don't even notice the effects of the purchase when looking at our bank balance. However, the implications of that one t-shirt are great, especially when over two billion t-shirts are sold annually. Cotton is very resource intensive. And the way the cotton is produced and made into a t-shirt can be either beneficial for the environment or have negative effects.

Every part of our fashion has a story behind it. There is a designer, a maker and a grower. Sometimes there was a person in the fields who took care of each plant and bud as the fluffy white balls of softness grew out of nowhere. Cotton can be grown in various ways — it can be fed and nurtured organically or with chemicals and pesticides. The soil that cotton emerged from could be healthy and brimming with nutrients, or just a simple seed forced to grow by human intervention. Cotton requires thousands of litres of water to grow. Water is a precious resource, and yet we don't think of all this or any of the other myriad issues when we see a rack of t-shirts in a store.

In this industrialised, global world, we are very disconnected from the process used to create our clothes. We may have greater choice and cheaper prices than years ago, but at what cost? Choice doesn't always dictate healthy outcomes. This means we need to be acting consciously and approaching fashion with a considered mindset.

Have you ever gone online and come across a video of someone sewing in the workroom of Chanel or Dior? The women in their white jackets, treating each pattern and garment like a priceless object? Like a treasure? I just love these videos — they invoke such respect for the process. These videos are a view into the process of an artist. There are makers around the world doing exactly the same beautiful work. There are makers in your own country who are dedicated to their craft, putting love into what they do with skill that has taken years to develop.

Why does this skill and craftsmanship matter? It is significant because the clothing produced has value, it contains the inspiration of a design, it holds years of skill represented in a single stitch. The stories of the people who make the clothes are contained within them. Often these people are part of a small business. Even if our garments aren't created by artisans, we can still choose pieces that are created by people who care, whose personal lives benefit as well as nature.

Each decision we make has an impact. We saw what happened in the world when everyone stopped because of Covid-19. The air cleared up in highly polluted areas like Shanghai and Delhi and animals started returning to places that had been overcrowded. Before this, even if we were aware of climate change, much of life continued as usual. When the world stopped, it became very obvious the impact that our day-to-day life was having on our environment as well as our experience of it.

To engage with fashion consciously means we need to be selective. This is a great thing. If we are used to purchasing a garment without thinking about it, it may feel uncomfortable to stop ourselves and ask whether we really need it or whether it's the best choice environmentally. However, when we are able to interrupt our habitual ways of doing things, we can then make decisions that will have greater impact and serve us for a longer period of time.

IT'S TIME TO ASK YOURSELF SOME QUESTIONS

Throughout this book some of the topics may prompt you to ask yourself questions. In doing this you will be hitting pause on old beliefs and habits to see if there are new ways of doing things. This is like taking a different route to work or cooking from a recipe we haven't used before. It requires a new level of awareness. And this means becoming conscious of what we have done before, choosing what resonates today, and making new decisions in the future.

Choosing consciously is beneficial for our resources. Our personal resources — money, time and energy — as well as the resources of the planet. Choosing consciously will make us question if we are doing things out of convention or if it's the way we want to be. For example, do you really like wearing polyester or do you buy it because it's cheaper? Do you feel good in polyester or does it make you sweat? If it's cheaper, what does that mean? Who and what does that impact? There are many questions we can ask to reorientate ourselves towards a better fashion experience.

Acting consciously is not just about what we buy. If we are to truly think differently about fashion it also relates to the clothing we currently own and wear. It starts with being honest with ourselves. I know it's not easy sometimes when you look in the mirror and wish the person looking back at you was taller, shorter, slimmer, younger, more confident, more ambitious ... and the list goes on.

Many people take a quick glance and then continue doing things the way they always have been. It's easy to accept things as okay even if you know you would like to look and feel different. Sometimes people don't know how to make a change, especially if they are happy with their appearance but would like to make better fashion decisions, including buying less and buying better. Sometimes the person they want to look like seems too far out of reach, and sometimes people have never really considered whether there is a better way to be more satisfied with their appearance.

What if this way of being is what is creating havoc in your wardrobe? What if it's your cloudy perception that makes you buy the wrong clothes? What if you could correct the way your perceive yourself when looking in the mirror with a few simple tweaks? What if it's not about becoming more of anything but about learning some simple tips and tricks that will bring out your natural beauty if you're a woman and charisma if you're a man (or vice versa if you'd prefer)?

To do this requires us to become conscious of the way we have been acting. The way we have chosen the garments that don't necessarily accentuate our best features. Being conscious also asks us to honour our resources, our money and time, as well as honouring ourselves.

Rethinking fashion and being honest with ourselves isn't painful. It's actually like a breath of fresh air once you learn how to find the right garments that accentuate your natural, wonderful self. It's also extremely refreshing to simplify your wardrobe experience to make it more in alignment with who you truly are. And so let's start here, with a clean slate. Realising that we can engage with fashion in new and satisfying ways. Realising that we can make uplifting, positive decisions that will not only bring out the best in us but also do greater good for the planet and the people who make our clothes.

CHAPTER 10

How do we make better decisions?

'I don't think *what you do* is enough anymore,
it's *how you do it* that is important.' — Javier Goyeneche

Now that we know the significance of making conscious choices, how do we actually make those decisions? How do we know what actions need to change?

We need to be able to distinguish between the things we are currently doing that are great and those that may need improvement. To make better decisions about our fashion, we need to take the time to assess every aspect of our relationship with fashion and ask how it can be more in alignment with ethical and environmental values. This means we look at:

- how we feel about the clothes we currently wear, what they are made of and how we treat them

- our knowledge about the brands we currently shop from and their practices

- our values and beliefs around leather and other animal skins, feathers and furs

- whether we currently buy from fast fashion and what we believe about it

- our values and habits to do with shopping.

By understanding our current values and actions, we can then choose to make different decisions. We can start to carve out a new way of thinking about fashion. We can use this knowledge to empower us. We make better decisions when we have enough knowledge and are willing to act differently.

Doing something new and different takes time in the beginning. It takes time to assimilate the new knowledge as well as physically adopting a new behaviour. In this fast-paced world we have become accustomed to quick, one-stop solutions. Click and collect, next-day delivery, free shipping, add-ons at the checkout. There are apps to employ someone to pick up a parcel and bring it to us, or to cook a meal and have it delivered. The trend has moved us towards cutting out the care in the process and just going from start to finish in the blink of an eye.

UNDERSTANDING THE OPTIONS

Recently when I visited my partner I came face to face with this and realised why it can be tempting to choose the easy option. As I walked into his apartment, there was a big plastic bag filled with clothes right in the doorway. After losing some weight and moving from the tropics of Cairns to Melbourne, which has four seasons in a day, he decided he needed a wardrobe revamp and finally made the jump to sort through his clothes and let some go. This bag was filled with shirts and other pieces of clothing.

Being in fashion, I always err on the side of caution and try not to make suggestions about what he should wear. He knows I'm not a fan of the floral shirts but we had to come to a compromise. We decided that florals stay but I'm not around when they are worn. So the bag did not contain florals, but it did have a whole lot of shirts that no longer fit him or that had lost their relevance.

My partner loathes getting rid of anything he has invested money in, especially those pieces that he hasn't worn much – it seems like such a waste to him. So there we were, staring at the bag of clothes in the hallway wondering what to do with it.

He said he would send the clothing to charity — this made me think about the implications. Depending on the state of the clothing, it could be resold in one of the charity's clothing stores, but what mostly happens is it's sent to landfill, incinerated or shipped to a developing country.

I really didn't like the thought of supporting a disposable mindset by dropping it off at a charity and letting them deal with it, and so I thought about how I could help. I thought about putting pieces on a resale website. It would take time to assess each item, clean it and press it, then photograph it. It would take at least a day to go through all of it. To be honest, it put me off. However, when I thought about the alternative — that I would be contributing to our textile waste problem — I needed to accept the challenge.

What I'm trying to point out here is that when we decide to make better decisions we need to take a look at all the options. We also need to find out what each of those imply, and then consciously choose the most ethical and environmental decision.

WHAT IS MOTIVATING YOU?

To make better decisions it's also good to understand our motivations. There are three reasons we can be motivated to choose our fashion differently:

- The first one is wanting to look and feel better. It's understanding how we actually want to get dressed each day. If we have pieces that we actually don't feel good in then it's not very uplifting. If we remember the way we feel in our best outfits and decide to choose in accordance with this feeling, it's more likely we will choose less and choose better.

- The second motivator towards making better decisions is for the environment. It's remembering the huge impact fashion has on the planet. It feels good to buy something you know has been made consciously with care, and perhaps with a slower but more respectful process.

- The third is being motivated by empathy and compassion towards the many people who make our clothes. When we keep a garment for years we are respecting the work that went into it. When we buy a garment that was made in ethical working conditions, we are supporting an ethical supply chain. We are ensuring a living wage for garment workers and artisans and also giving back to humanity.

We make better decisions by asking better questions. Or any questions at all, sometimes. Making better decisions and seeing a greater impact takes time. But if we stay true to our vision for change, bit by bit we will create it. To make better decisions, let's assess our values, what we hold dear in our own lives, and how we can live more in accordance with those principals.

CHAPTER 11

What are we really trying to achieve?

'I believe we are on our way to a better world.'
— Carmen Busquets

WELLBEING

What is the outcome we are after when we talk about rethinking fashion? This is the question I have thought about a lot and it kept coming back to one word: wellbeing. It is wellbeing for ourselves, our environment and the lives of others.

As I mentioned earlier, we all have the desire to be better, and I believe what underpins this is a natural inclination to want to experience greater levels of wellbeing. Within us there is an innate need for balance, wholeness and equilibrium. When we recognise that something is off, that it doesn't feel right, whether we know it or not we are always trying to restore that balance.

What is wellbeing? It is an experience of wholeness. It is a state where our body and mind are in balance. It is a recognition of something greater than our individual needs and desires. On a personal level it is a feeling of connection and a positive awareness of something greater than ourselves.

In the Indian tradition of yoga, the ancient scriptures recognise that our inner world and outer world are one and the same. That the way we are on the inside determines our life on the outside. I think this is true on a practical level as well as a spiritual one. If you think about the way we perceive things as individuals, it all comes down to our individual preferences and our subconscious beliefs and attitudes. Whenever we shift a belief we see things differently and act differently.

True wellbeing is a state beyond individual beliefs and preferences – it is a balance of the body, the heart and the mind. And wellbeing of the environment and nature is just as important as our own wellbeing. It's very obvious that as human civilisation has eroded nature we are experiencing greater fluctuations in weather patterns. As the world's population increases it places greater stress on our environment. We can no longer afford to act and move about our lives without thinking about our impact on the planet.

But where does this all get us? Rather than looking to acquire more, be more and have more, why don't we look to create a life where we are truly content with what we have and who we are? Imagine if each person around the world was focused on simpler, more satisfying experiences. If we were committed to our own wellbeing as well as that of the planet. And I'm not talking about fluffy wellbeing like going to a spa. I'm talking about satisfaction at a deep level. And this comes through experiences and practices that meet our deepest values and needs.

Agreeing to put this into practice means elevating our awareness. It will require us to set a higher bar for ourselves and our life. For example, something that is very simple and mundane: if you are used to buying cheap clothing because you feel you save money and clothing is not worth that much anyway, what if you made a shift and committed to buying yourself some clothing of better quality that would last longer? I bet you would feel better in those clothes and maybe even stand taller. And this would not be the only benefit. Those better quality purchases, if you kept them longer, would hopefully mean you would buy less clothing over all and then this would mean less impact for the environment. And you'd save money. Can you see how this elevated awareness has benefits for all?

THE SIMPLE LIFE

This belief about wellbeing is something that I have personally experienced on a very deep level. In 1998 when I was in my late 20s, I made a very radical choice for someone of my age to move to India. This was a time when my friends were all developing their careers and pursuing their passions with gusto, and I decided to go against the norm by visiting the land and true home of meditation and yoga. I had been practising meditation for years by myself in Melbourne, as well as studying the ancient texts of India which speak about cultivating a more conscious and disciplined life.

What was it that drew me to India? It was a deep sense that the knowledge and experiences I would have there would bring about personal growth that was priceless. I knew it was the opportunity of a lifetime.

At first I moved there with the idea I would be there for six months, but as the time rolled around I realised I wanted to stay longer. In the beginning it took some time to adjust to such an extremely different culture to my own. I describe living in India to my friends like having to put aside everything we have known in Western countries to understand and relate to the culture.

Every morning I would wake up at 4am to meditate. I loved the monsoon time the most because of the sound of the rain and the smell of tropical flowers like jasmine as I walked across marble floors to the meditation room. Over time, as I studied the ancient texts of India and practised meditation, I found a deeper and independent sense of wellbeing. It wasn't reliant on circumstance or what I was doing that day. It was a very buoyant and concrete experience. In a place without TV, cell phones or internet, or the constant barrage of advertising from magazines and billboards, I was becoming very content.

As I practised a very disciplined, focused and simple way of life, it became more and more uplifting. This experience made me want to keep growing, keep learning, and doing whatever I could to maintain this state. How amazing to think that this experience of fulfilment came from one decision years earlier to practise meditation.

Living in India provided me with an elevated outlook on life. I found that the simpler my life was, the more fulfilled I felt. I was happy, and also found that time with friends was also more joyful. I truly understood that wellbeing comes from within, and it came through experience. All of this without buying anything new or pursuing a continuous stream of new experiences thinking they would give me that state.

The state of wellbeing comes from within, but we must cultivate it. We must practise the qualities that we wish to have in our life. Once we start making choices towards greater wellbeing, it inspires us to want to see this wellbeing elsewhere.

By picking up this book you have demonstrated a desire to make decisions that are congruent with your values. To bring about a positive change in our lives we need to commit to greater wellbeing for ourselves and others as well as the health of our planet overall.

PART III

The state of fashion

'We need to be honest with each other and talk about what's difficult.'

—Eva Kruse

WHEN OUR PARENTS were growing up, fashion was a much simpler affair, there was less on offer, and fashion businesses offered better quality clothing. If clothing was imported then it was a big deal, and discovering these luxurious pieces was just as impressive as the price. Things are so much different now. The fashion industry has sped up and created so much choice that we are now drowning in clothes. This is both literally as we open our wardrobes and figuratively in terms of the amount of items being produced.

As a result of this globalised and accessible fashion, the environment is suffering and people are being taken advantage of. There are myriad unmistakeable issues that now need to be confronted. The fashion industry has been operating in an unsustainable manner for many years, and yet it has continued full steam, and some companies are still increasing in capacity.

We are at a point where this momentum can no longer continue and its effects cannot be ignored. It is no longer an option to continue operating in the same way. A new approach must be taken. In the coming chapters you will discover the current state of the industry and why it must change.

CHAPTER 12

Our perception of value has changed over time

'If everyone started to question the way we consume,
we would see a radically different fashion paradigm.'
— Carry Somers

My relationship with clothing and fabrics has always been connected with a process. As a child, I would watch my mother make her own clothes. I would also watch her spend hour after hour weaving beautiful hand-crafted fabrics on a loom. In today's world, it's very rare that we would have the time to make our own clothes. When we buy clothes all we have to do is walk into a store and select something from a rack or order on a screen, but do we have any connection to how that garment was made or where it came from?

When my mother spent time weaving, she would have the loom set up in the living room. You can get small looms to make things like a tea-towel sized wall hanging, or you can use a much bigger version that makes blanket-sized pieces – this is what my mother had. This thing was so big that it almost took up the entire space of the living room where she worked.

The wool or yarn she used had been made and dyed carefully by hand. This was the '70s and '80s, so this lifestyle was a flow-on from the hippy era where everything was handmade and hand grown. I remember watching my mother make these yarns from scratch. She would buy a big bag of woollen fleece which still had the fresh smell of lanolin and being shorn.

She separated the wool into hand-sized amounts and put it between two brushes – called carding brushes – which would relax and comb the fibres.

Then she would hold the brushed fleece and move it through a spinning wheel until it rolled into a yarn. Afterwards, I remember her taking the yarn and dyeing it with natural dyes of gum leaf and other beautiful natural colours. There were big copper pots she used to dye the wool before hanging it out to dry. The whole thing took days.

When the yarn was dry, the weaving began. Pieces of yarn were threaded horizontally to create the base of the project, and then other yarns were woven vertically across them. It's a time-consuming process but also a beautiful one. I loved to watch her projects come to life. There was one particular piece she made which was a favourite of mine. It was a beautiful, natural-coloured piece of browns and creams, and was so soft to touch. Years later as an adult my mother gave this piece to me, and it has become a treasure and valued piece.

THE REAL VALUE OF A GARMENT

To me, the real value of any piece of work like this or any garment lies in the time, skill and workmanship behind it. The beauty of a garment lies in the hours of creativity and endeavour. For any garment that is worthwhile, someone has spent years of their life developing the patternmaking, tailoring, dressmaking and designing skills to make it come to life. Not to mention the hours of work it takes to sew something that will be well made and last for years to come.

Creating garments in this way is far different from the clothing produced by fast fashion. Fast fashion pumps out trend-based clothing in large quantities for very cheap prices. They also put new items into store every couple of weeks, which has created a whole new appetite for the new. Fast fashion has changed how the average person values clothes.

In the beginning when these trendy cheap items first came out, we all fell for it because it was so exciting. However, it didn't take long to find out just how cheap these clothes actually were. They would quickly fall apart at the seams or go out of shape, and we would only manage a few wears out of them.

Unfortunately, the strength and power of these cheap brands is holding strong and people are buying into it. Other fashion brands who produce clothes on a traditional model only a few times a year are trying to compete by producing more clothes more regularly. The thing is that you can't create quality clothing at this fast pace; the two don't go together.

The constant influx of new clothing has also created a culture of discounting, as brands try to sell the 'old' stock — which is really only a few weeks or months old. Over the last few years discounting has become the norm, and it's almost expected that you will be able to buy what you are looking for on sale. It's a real debacle, because this expectation also decreases the value of clothing in the perceptions of society.

Unfortunately, as the big fast fashion brands dominate, local brands have seen a decline in customers. Over the years I have seen many boutiques and independent fashion brands close their doors because of this changing landscape. One of my favourite boutiques in Melbourne has been struggling over recent years. They used to be one of the leading boutiques, where you could buy a designer piece that was well made and on the leading edge of fashion. But recently I've had many conversations with the owner of this boutique about the negative impact fast fashion and globalisation has had on their business.

This struggle for relevance is because of a change in values, not only of price but also in how people prefer to shop: online. A globalised marketplace has meant we now shop for the best bargain of a particular brand and have global options to compare. Local brands are suffering, and to me this is a real pity because some of the best creativity comes from smaller independent brands.

One upside of the time we live in is that independent designers do have the ability to start their own fashion business with minimal investment compared to years ago. They can promote themselves freely on Instagram and build a following at a realistic pace. So in some ways there are advantages of the time we are in, but on the whole, there is a big struggle to bring back the value of a garment in the average consumer's mind.

WE NEED A NEW MODEL

This disposable mindset means we are even more removed from the design process and the energy and resources it takes to make clothing. The thing is that the world doesn't need more cheap clothes. We need a new model where the value of clothing is honoured once again.

When we look at the tag inside a garment and it says made in India, China or Vietnam, what does that even mean? Most of the time we don't really know. Was the whole thing made in China? Where did the material come from? Who did the design? There is a whole ecosystem behind the creation of a garment, and it can either contribute to the environment and humanity or it can detract from it.

What disheartens me is to hear people talking about their fashion purchases with no intention to keep them for long, or with any strategy in mind. We can no longer afford to buy clothing without thinking about the impact. We need to be thinking with longevity in mind. If people had a strategy behind their clothes with the intention to keep them for a long time, they would be more considered about each and every purchase. Buying just for the sake of newness can be done till the cows come home, but what real value has it added to our wardrobes, our personal style or to people's lives?

We can change this so our purchases do mean something and our actions also mean something. Imagine buying a garment from a designer knowing that the fabrics used were produced with minimal impact on the environment. That the entire process was without pesticides or chemical use. Imagine as you buy the product instore or online you are told in a very caring and authentic way about the people who made your clothes, how much they get paid, and the quality of their working conditions. Imagine seeing a video of them sewing garments as well as working with the designer to make sure the fit and form of the garment was perfect. Wouldn't that create a whole different sense of value?

To turn the tide on fashion and shift to a more responsible model, we can do our part to buy from brands who communicate even a small part of their process like this. When we make a big purchase – like a car, for example — we take a lot into account: the make, the model, whether it suits our lifestyle, how long it will last, and the quality of the brand and materials. It really should be like this with our clothes.

Bringing back the value to clothing is not about buying *more*. It's actually about loving what we already have, and buying only in a considered way. It's enjoying the beauty and longevity of the items. It means owning only clothing that we truly do need, love and feel great in, so much so that we don't think need to think about buying new pieces.

When my mother was a child, up until she was a young woman all her clothes were made by my grandmother. Clothes were valued in this era, and buying and following trends didn't exist. Wardrobes were small and clothes were made to last. This means that when they made these clothes, they paid attention to all the details like fit, fabric and the structure of the garment. They were made to suit their individual shape and style — why would you want to wear them if they didn't suit you? And after so much effort, it had to be worthwhile.

Purchasing a garment has to mean more now because of the state that the environment is in. Because of the way fast fashion has changed the landscape of fashion. It's time to get back to the old ways of doing things. We can have fewer clothes, and they can still be beautiful. If you buy with consideration and more of a strategy, you can build a collection of incredible garments. You will be impressed and inspired by how many options to restyle you will have within your very own wardrobe.

CHAPTER 13

What does 'sustainability' actually mean?

'A product always has an impact.' — August Bard Bringéus

'Sustainability' is a word that gets used and overused all the time. In some ways, I feel we are becoming immune to it. We assume it's purely relating to the environment, when in reality it's so much more. Trying to define what sustainability means is challenging for all.

When I think about this issue, these are the things I'm thinking about:

- climate change
- sourcing materials
- manufacturing
- farming processes
- biodiversity loss
- water usage
- chemical use and pollution
- business practices
- economic impact
- diminishing natural and human resources
- consumption and waste
- transportation and its carbon footprint
- packaging.

Let's have a look at each of these.

CLIMATE CHANGE

We are all aware of the growing and urgent conversation around climate change. You may not be as aware that the fashion industry has a huge role to play in this issue. The fashion industry accounts for approximately 10% of global carbon emissions; that's more than the aviation and shipping industries combined (Ellen MacArthur Foundation). The fashion industry's carbon emissions continue to increase, even though scientists say the amount of carbon dioxide in the atmosphere already exceeds a safe limit.

SOURCING MATERIALS

Not all fabrics and other materials in the fashion industry are equal. Some are sourced and produced with minimal harm to the environment and others without care at all. The sourcing of materials includes farming practices and fibre production. Many conventional farming practices use huge amounts of chemicals. These chemicals are also used in the creation of fabrics right across the process. Sourcing materials impacts on water use, and creates huge carbon emissions depending on the methods.

MANUFACTURING

Fashion exists at such a large scale that it's difficult to conceive the amount of energy, water and resources needed for production. The production process also creates a huge amount of textile and chemical waste.

For the manufacturing of fashion garments to be sustainable, they need to be created with economically-sound processes that minimise environmental impact. These processes also need to be able to conserve energy and natural resources.

FARMING PROCESSES

Large-scale farming is required to feed the growing rate of production of the fashion industry. Unfortunately, the focus is on quantity and speed rather than producing with integrity. Large-scale farming has led to the breakdown and destruction of fertile land. The production of crops, animal furs and skins often strips the land of nutrients and soil integrity, leaving it bare. Farming processes have also contributed to the loss of ancient and endangered forests. These practices also require vast amounts of water.

BIODIVERSITY LOSS

Biodiversity is the variety of life on our planet, and is essential for it to thrive and survive. Clare Press, a sustainability advocate, refers to The World Economic Forum's description of biodiversity as 'the most fundamental building block of nature'. They say that it's 'the variability and abundance of living organisms and their habitats'. It's the way plants and animals live in a community and interact together in a specific environment. Biodiversity is the lifeblood of our planet.

Fashion is an agriculture-based industry – it relies on farming, forests and animals for all of its products. The farming of livestock, cotton and other fibres has been directly linked to the loss of delicate ecosystems as well as the habitat of many species of wildlife. We have truly taken nature for granted.

WATER USAGE

The water used to produce fabrics is immense. This includes farming and machine processes. According to the Ellen MacArthur Foundation, textile production uses around *93 billion cubic metres* of water annually. This is the equivalent of 37 million Olympic swimming pools, or about 17 Sydney Harbours. With over one billion people on the planet who currently lack access to clean drinking water, you can see the unethical and unsustainable role that fashion plays.

CHEMICAL USE AND POLLUTION

The clothes we wear, unless they are organic, contain many more chemicals than you or I would like to think about. Chemicals are used all along the fashion supply chain, and contribute to some of the highest levels of air and water pollution. Up to 8000 chemicals can be used in the production of textiles. This includes farming and the growth of natural fibres like cotton, linen and silk.

Did you know that more chemicals are used in cotton production than any other crop? Cotton is always promoted as a soft, appealing and natural fabric. However, unless it is organic, the path it takes before being turned into a t-shirt is hazardous.

Chemicals are also used in dyeing, printing, treating, steaming, pressing and finishing fabrics and garments. Fabric dyes are some of the biggest contributors to pollution on the planet. In China, it's said that you can tell what the colours of the next fashion season will be by the colour of the rivers.

One of the areas where chemical use is most concerning in the fashion industry is within the tanneries that treat leather. This is hazardous environmentally, as well as for the people who do the work. It takes a lot of unnatural processes and many chemicals to turn a biodegradable, breathable product into something that will stand the test of time.

BUSINESS PRACTICES

Many fashion supply chain and business practices are inefficient, leaving millions of dollars on the table. As the conversation around the impact of the fashion industry is growing, so too are the studies which show that converting to more ecologically friendly processes in textile and garment production would actually save money as well as decreasing the impact on the environment.

ECONOMIC IMPACT

The model for any fashion business to survive is based on a projection of growth year on year. Many businesses are focused on financial growth alone, without regard for the environmental or humanitarian impact, and this is truly not a sustainable model.

There is also huge economic imbalance within the supply chain. While leaders and top creatives receive high financial reward for their work, the hands-on areas like the factories and garment construction are often squeezed for profit. With garment workers often paid below the minimum living wage, the negative economic impact extends beyond the factory walls. These garment workers return to their communities unable to contribute. There is a huge disparity of wealth distribution among the fashion supply chain, not to mention a lack of transparency around pricing and value.

DIMINISHING NATURAL AND HUMAN RESOURCES

The fashion industry is one of the most resource-intensive industries in the world. It relies on both human and natural resources, and these are all either declining or finite.

When a fashion collection is created, the entire process — from the creation to transportation to maintenance and use of a garment — is reliant of finite fossil fuels. It's unsustainable. Textile production, especially for synthetics, uses a huge amount of non-renewable natural resources. Specifically, according to the Ellen MacArthur Foundation, it uses 98 million tonnes of oil globally each year.

The diminishing of resources also relates to artisanal and hand-based skills across the globe, which are disappearing as fast-paced manufacturing increases. Artisanal skills are the foundation of many intricate and unique garments, and without them we would all look the same.

CONSUMPTION AND WASTE

Clothing production continues to increase at an unrealistic and unsustainable pace. And the problem is that on average people are keeping items for shorter and shorter timeframes. Since 2000, the production of clothing has doubled, and on average we are wearing items for half as long (Centre for Sustainable Fashion). When this clothing is discarded, most of it is ending up in landfill or being incinerated, which means we have a huge environmental problem.

According to the Ellen MacArthur Foundation, more than US$500 billion of value is lost every year due to clothing underutilisation and the lack of recycling. Most governments and cities around the world have either no solution or minimal options for textile recycling. The lack of solutions mean that day after day the amount of textile waste is increasing in its impact.

TRANSPORTATION AND ITS CARBON FOOTPRINT

The world is the market when it comes to sourcing materials in the fashion industry. In order to find the perfect fabrics, buttons, ribbons and so on, fashion brands purchase them from around the globe. The transportation of all of these products creates incredible amounts of CO_2 emissions, damaging the atmosphere.

And once an item has been created, it needs to be transported around the globe once again, which also pollutes the atmosphere with carbon emissions. With most clothing being made in countries far away from where the designs were conceived, it really is a huge problem. As well as the production process, think about ecommerce and the amount of carbon emissions created flying purchased goods around the world to their destination, and sometimes back if clothing is returned.

PACKAGING

Imagine ordering a belt online and receiving it in a box the size of a small coffee table, with plastic wrap and packaging bubbles all around. You open up the box, take out all the fillers, and there is a second tiny box the size of your hand containing the belt. This packaging example is common. If you multiply that by the millions of ecommerce orders every year, imagine the waste it creates.

This is just part of the packaging dilemma. There is also packaging involved in the transportation of raw materials, the fabrics, clothing from factory to store, and the list goes on. Then think about all the promotional material, tags, labels and more.

Packing overall needs to be fundamentally redesigned – about 30% of plastic packaging will never be reused or recycled (Ellen MacArthur Foundation).

* * *

When we look at sustainability under all these categories we see the true complexity. Fashion draws on a huge amount of natural resources and is extremely polluting. This is why the issue is hard to define – it covers so much ground. Today there is a much bigger meaning.

CHAPTER 14

The reality of sustainability fatigue

'Sustainability has been a very, very overused word.'
— Stella McCartney

Now that we know the sheer depth and enormity of what's involved, it's so easy to see why people have sustainability fatigue. It's almost as if the term 'sustainability' needs to be redefined, so we can understand what it really means. It's possible we have become so used to hearing about this issue that it's like living next to a train line: over time you don't even hear the noise.

Of course, we all care and we want to do better, but at some point it can feel a bit overwhelming. Why would we be fatigued with such an important issue? Climate change and environmental degradation affects each of us, so wouldn't we want to do our part?

One reason we are at a point of sustainability fatigue is because we are often removed from the implications. For the most part, these issues don't impact us in an immediate way or in our day-to-day life. When we purchase a garment, it's not as if we get a glimpse into all the processes it took to get there. When we throw a garment away, it's a bit of 'out of sight, out of mind'.

As customers, we aren't being shown what sustainability really means by the brands we love. The number of brands who demonstrate how it is being implemented in their businesses is still in the minority. This poses another question: are sustainable practices really being implemented, and at what level?

HOW DO I START MAKING BETTER CHOICES?

Having the knowledge is the first step in each of us making a difference, but making the right decisions in the moment takes effort. I recently experienced this when a friend of mine was looking for some more sweaters for winter. She bought a cashmere sweater from a fast fashion brand a year before and loved it. Not wanting it to wear out from wearing it all the time, she jumped online to buy some more and was stoked to find that they were half price.

Sharing the love, she sent a text to let me know. I jumped on board and went to the site to purchase some of these gorgeous sweaters for myself. Now, cashmere at full price from a fast fashion brand will be unethical in itself, but when it's sold for much less than it should be you can imagine the loss of value. Most cashmere is produced in unsustainable and unethical ways and is creating a huge environmental problem. And unless it is collected from goats on a very small farm in Nepal, it's likely you are buying into the problem.

After looking through the colours and styles of these sweaters for a few minutes, I stopped myself and realised what was happening. Even though the design and the price were very appealing, I felt uneasy. I just couldn't bring myself to purchase. It took some personal will, but I remembered my commitment to a more sustainable and ethical approach to fashion and said *no* to something that at first glance was so appealing. I also remembered that there are many ways to find beautiful woollen sweaters, that I could shop vintage and buy designer items from a few seasons ago, or I could do my research and find brands that do align with my values.

The reality of fatigue in this situation was that it felt so much easier to buy the option in front of me. It seemed like a bigger effort to have to find something in the price range I wanted to pay, while also being happy with the design and environmental impact.

But once I had made the decision, I felt content. I had pried myself away from temptation and chosen the good.

ALL THESE QUESTIONS ...

When trying to navigate the fashion landscape, questions can pop up like, where do I start? How do I find the right brands to buy from, and how can I trust that they are actually doing the right thing? You may ask, how can I find beautiful, elegant garments that are also made with environmentally methods? Maybe you are unsure about the higher price tag as a result of something being made locally and sustainably.

You may also ask, how will I find the type of clothing I like while still being ethical and environmentally responsible?

All these questions contribute to sustainability fatigue. It can seem like there is just too much to think about — it can be confusing to sift through all the information and choices to make an informed decision.

One of the first champions of a more sustainable fashion industry was Stella McCartney. Stella has been a champion for animal rights and sustainably-made clothing since the inception of her brand in 2001. Her brand has incorporated ethical and sustainable principles across the business from the beginning, and is continually working to improve and refine them.

Because of her profile — she is the daughter of English singer and songwriter Sir Paul McCartney, as well as being a talented and successful fashion designer in her own right — Stella McCartney has managed to make a lot of people stand up and take notice. Industry professionals and those of us purchasing new garments are being influenced by her stance. A prominent, active voice like Stella's is what we need more of to show us what sustainability truly looks like in a business and how it creates a positive impact.

TRACEABILITY

One thing we can do to cut through the noise of the conversation is to engage with fashion brands directly. This starts by finding out how they demonstrate sustainable actions. If a brand is truly committed to reducing their impact on the environment, it will be shown in the *doing* not in the *talking*. From this doing they will be able to show you how they are producing beautiful garments which have the least impact on the environment. This is called 'traceability'.

Traceability can only take place when there is transparency. And this is what we need to look for so that we can have confidence that good practices are truly being implemented. Transparency is very much linked to sustainability, and is key to being able to demonstrate sustainable actions when you buy a product from that brand.

* * *

Sustainability fatigue is due to overwhelm and not being able to sort the wheat from the chaff. And this is why there needs to be clear markers and signs of a sustainable, ethical brand when we look at their profile. These are topics we will get into in the next couple of chapters. Just know that this is a real and timely issue; we do need to take it seriously but we need to know what to look for.

CHAPTER 15

Not all companies act the same

'Refrain from buying from brands with questionable sustainable practices.' — Bandana Tewari

In the past, fashion brands weren't questioned about their ethical stance or their sustainability practices. Actually, the real problem was that they weren't questioned at all. Of course, now we live in a world where questions are asked and transparency is expected, and commitment to ethical and sustainable practices is demanded. So, how do you know which fashion brands are doing the right thing and which aren't?

Up until recently the truly sustainable, ethical and beautiful brands were in the minority. I mean, who wants to wear a hessian sack to a cocktail event no matter how sustainable it is? I'd rather stay home and watch Netflix. But sustainable clothing has evolved. The issues the industry faces have reached fever pitch, and we are seeing more and more brands coming on board with an appealing and authentic offering.

Not all fashion brands are equal, and you need to be on the lookout. If you don't know how to look for the information then it's likely it will go unnoticed, and if a fashion brand isn't acting ethically they will remain unaccountable.

The best place to start looking for information is on a company website. If they really are committed to change they will have obvious navigation links on their home page. If they have a section devoted to sustainability then you know that they are making an effort (although look out for 'greenwashing', which we'll look at later).

Unfortunately, this is where it can become even more confusing, as every business has a different way of promoting their activity. For example, there could be a brand that is making an effort with organic textiles but is still having their clothing produced in unethical factories where labor conditions are questionable. Would you buy from them? I wouldn't.

It really is a bit of a minefield out there to be able to ascertain just how far down the transparency journey a company is. And this is where you and I need to decide just what we will and won't accept. We need to decide whether we are prepared to put our money behind our values.

At what point will you be prepared to walk away if a company isn't sharing enough information about their practices?

IT'S UP TO US WHAT WE ACCEPT

There are two things we need to navigate. The first one is where a brand sits on the sliding scale of transparency and accountability. The second is that we need to be very clear on our position in all of this. There is a lot of grey, and it's up to us what we accept.

It takes time and strategy for a fashion brand to change its practices if they weren't sustainably focused before. This means we need to be mindful as we choose who to shop from. In your local area there may not be many options, and so it's probably a question of choosing the lesser of two evils; for example, buying an organic t-shirt over a non-organic one. Or you may decide to choose a t-shirt made of conventional cotton which was grown and sourced locally as well as being made locally. This choice would mean you are choosing minimal greenhouse gas emissions which is also a positive choice.

On the other hand, you can take a complete and pure approach to the issue and decide right here and now that you will only engage with brands who are 100% transparent and ethical in their practices. If you do choose this approach, know that there will be an adjustment period. It's a great one though, because it will mean you will be elevating your whole experience of fashion.

As the sustainability and ethical issues have become more obvious to me, I have realised just how much of an effort I need to make to adjust my own approach to fashion. It can be hard to make a decision when there is a brand you have been buying from for years and they are not disclosing anything about their working conditions, sourcing or waste management. It then becomes an ethical question. Will you continue to support them? When you have bought into a brand's aesthetic and style over many years, it can be difficult to change.

The main message here is to choose your side of the fence. Decide how you are going to approach this. There is no hard and fast rule. Be on the lookout for brands who tout sustainability and be prepared to dig deeper. Don't stop until you have a conclusive answer. Only then can you truly make a decision.

CHAPTER 16

What is 'greenwashing'?

'Unclear naming is luring customers into a false sense that their action is doing "good".' — August Bard Bringéus

As the sustainability movement has grown over time, much like sustainability fatigue, there is another confusing topic to potentially catch people off guard. There is a lot of noise out there and much of it lacks substance. In your own shopping trips you may have seen the terms 'eco-friendly' or 'conscious' being used liberally. But what do they actually mean? This is where we begin to head into grey territory.

You will be happy to know there is a term for this, and the lack of clarity is not your fault — the term is 'greenwashing'.

So, what exactly is it? Greenwashing is when a brand's marketing messages around sustainability are contrary to its business practices. An obvious example would be if a fast fashion brand promoted the fact that they were launching an eco-friendly label when all they did was release a single line of organic t-shirts. This is a deliberately vague and misleading statement.

These kinds of statements are a huge problem in the fashion industry. They are also a major contributor towards sustainability fatigue. The greenwashing issue has prompted brands whose entire business is built on sustainability to reject the term altogether, and I don't blame them. Many of them prefer to demonstrate their practices and be transparent about their supply chain, which speaks for itself.

Greenwashing is an issue that lessens the impact of any sincere progress that brands are making towards a positive environmental and humanitarian contribution. Greenwashing statements also make it hard to see the forest for the trees, and define who is authentic and who is not. The main thing you should be looking for is that a brand is truly showing you the impact they are making through their business practices. Sustainability is no longer an option; it is expected.

It's easy to be misled by images and statements that allude to sustainable practices. For example, a woman I know recently sent me a link to the website of a fashion brand who she said is doing great work in this space. She pointed out that the navigation menu on their website had a tab dedicated to sustainability.

After looking through the website, I checked an industry body that classifies fashion brands into a sustainability rating based on numerous certifications schemes, standards and independent ratings, as well as information directly disclosed by the brand itself. When I checked this company on their website, the rating told a different tale. It was shown that their practices were substandard. It mentioned that even though they spoke about where their factories were, there was no disclosure about the working conditions. Nor was there any clear information about how their fabrics were sourced or made.

This example illustrated to me the differences in information that is out there, and how we must become good at spotting the real deal. A brand must have sustainability built into its strategy all the way through its business. This means they have either started the business founded on a model of long-term viability, or if they have been around for some time and need to adjust, they are implementing these practices in ongoing stages.

HOW TO SPOT TRUE SUSTAINABILITY AND STEER CLEAR OF GREENWASHING

If you want to be sure of the true position a fashion brand takes on sustainability, there are numerous things you can look out for.

Ignore the marketing messages

The first rule of thumb should be to ignore the marketing fluff. These are terms like 'conscious collection', 'eco-friendly', 'green collection', or even just 'sustainable', believe it or not. These slogans are often misleading. For example, just because a company promotes their organic cotton t-shirts doesn't mean they were made in a factory with ethical working conditions. Rather than a slogan, look to see if they are showing you a timeline all the way through the process that demonstrates their practices.

Head to the website

The best place to start is the company website. At first glance you should be able to see some obvious information displaying their sustainable practices. Many brands have a dedicated tab for sustainability, but do not stop there. Dig deep, because you will want to see more than just a mission statement about caring for the environment for example, which could just be greenwashing.

Remember that using the term 'sustainability' on a website does not necessarily denote ethical and positive environmental practices. When you dig deeper, you will want to be able to read about the wholistic approach of the business. They should have multiple ways of demonstrating their practices, and the site should contain clear statistics and targets that are being measured, as well as industry certifications.

Find reliable statistics

A company that has truly embedded and embraced sustainability will be able to show you statistics which demonstrate how they have reduced their impact. Many companies are working to do this year on year, and set bold targets which they display on their website. For example:

> In spring/summer 2020 we used 40% deadstock (from a previous collection) fabrics in our collection and aim to use 80% by 2021.
> In spring/summer 2020 the remaining 60% of our fabrics were organic cotton and were sourced from fair trade suppliers.

These brands will be holding themselves accountable. Any brand that is committed to transparency will be able to show you this information.

For a brand to be considered truly sustainable it would need to show you targets across multiple areas of the business. This could be all or a combination of the following:

- water usage

- recyclable materials

- energy efficiency

- carbon emissions

- land regeneration

- waste production and management

- chemical use.

Examine their certifications

There are many industry bodies that brands use to benchmark their level of sustainability. You can look for any accreditation or logos that show you they meet industry standards. For example, there are different certifications for when a factory has been audited for healthy work practices. Organic cotton and fabric sometimes has its own certification. Some certifications are local accreditations, and some are globally used and recognised.

If a company is using industry standards and certifications they will be displayed on their website. Standards like those used for organic cotton will often be displayed on garment tags as well.

CHAPTER 17

The sheer amount of waste

'Waste, at the end of the day, is a design flaw.
It doesn't exist in nature.' —Gabriela Hearst

On holiday in Tasmania, I walk down a path surrounded by native scrub and step onto the pristine white beach. The colour of the sand is something you can't see anywhere else. There's something about the light in this part of the world which magnifies the already albino sand.

Looking out at the ocean, the view is also stunningly beautiful – the water is a mix of turquoise and cerulean blue and is crystal clear. I begin to walk on the empty beach. It stretches to a beautiful cove surrounded by rocks. I walk and walk, enjoying the sensation of the sand on my feet, the warmth of the sunshine and the sounds of the waves. There is still nobody around. It's truly the most stunning beach.

As I get close to the cove at the end of my walk, I notice something in the sand because it's so out of place. I walk up and see two plastic drink bottles squashed into the sand, not far from what had obviously been someone enjoying a fire on the beach at night.

I was stunned. How could someone not understand what a unique and rare gift it is to stand on a long stretch of beach like this, pristine and untouched? How could they leave toxic plastic bottles sitting there waiting to be washed into the ocean?

Wouldn't it be fantastic if this sense of disgust I experienced after finding those plastic bottles was also felt by leaders of the fashion industry towards its own waste? When they found out their companies were also polluting our precious planet in obvious and not so obvious ways?

What would be more impressive would be if this disbelief motivated them to commit to transforming their practices, regardless of the cost. A commitment that in time would see all design start with waste management practices in mind.

BY THE NUMBERS

Obviously, the following statistics are not pretty. While I share these statistics, please be mindful that it's very hard to assess numbers like this because it's all dependent on disclosure by fashion brands and the depth of the research. Still, these figures are a realistic view of the damage being created:

- Every second, the equivalent of one garbage truck of textiles is landfilled or burned (Ellen MacArthur).

- Clothing production doubled between 2000 and 2014 and items were worn half as much as before (McKinsey).

- The fashion industry produces 20% of global wastewater (UNEP).

- Clothes release half a million tonnes of microfibres into the ocean every year, equivalent to more than 50 billion plastic bottles (Ellen MacArthur).

- The average number of times a garment is worn before it ceases to be used has decreased by 36% compared to 15 years ago (Circular Fibres Initiative).

- Currently, 87% of material used for clothing production is landfilled or incinerated after its final use, representing a lost opportunity of more than US$100 billion annually, coupled with negative environmental impacts (Ellen MacArthur Foundation).

- Less than 1% of material used to produce clothing is recycled into new clothing (Ellen MacArthur Foundation).

- Each year in the United States alone, US$390 billion and five billion pounds worth of merchandise are sent to landfill (Optoro 2018 impact report).

We are so far from a waste-free fashion industry. In fact, it is one of the biggest contributors to landfill and environmental pollution. Each part of the fashion supply chain is compromised, from the sourcing of raw materials to the design stage, garment manufacturing, right up until these items reach our wardrobes.

The waste caused by textile disposal is huge, and a majority of the problem has been caused by the overproduction of the fast fashion industry and the average person's insatiable desire for the new. This is highlighted by the fact that the average Australian buys about 27 kilograms of textiles per year, and disposes of about 23 kilograms per year (Australian Bureau of Statistics).

Where do these discarded items go? Mostly to landfill or incineration. A lot of secondhand stores reject clothing from fast fashion brands because of the sheer quantity being dropped off weekly. It is also poor quality and has a low resale value. This clothing used to be shipped offshore to places like China and Africa, but now even these countries do not want it and we are being left with a huge waste problem.

Fast fashion has been a major contributor to the waste issue, creating hundreds of thousands of garments every few weeks. A large majority of this clothing is created out of manmade materials – mostly polyester. In fact, 70% of the clothes we buy are made of polyester. This cheap polyester clothing is one of the biggest waste issues in the fashion industry. It is not made to last, sewn with minimal attention to detail, and it falls apart quickly. Because polyester is a type of plastic, it doesn't break down, so once it's thrown away it will take hundreds of years to biodegrade, if at all.

WHAT A WASTE

Can you imagine buying a designer dress, taking it home, and then throwing it in a burning fire? Well, this is essentially what the fashion label Burberry did in 2017. It was widely reported that the luxury brand burned more than US$36.5 million worth of clothes, which critics say was a way of maintaining product scarcity and brand exclusivity. This was not the only time; incinerating unsold stock had been an annual practice at Burberry for at least five years until it came to light.

Unfortunately, Burberry was not the only company contributing to the industry's dirty little secret. Incinerating clothes is a practice that was said to be widespread in the industry. After this news came out in the media, Burberry committed to stop burning surplus stock, but it has left a lingering smoke of distaste and distrust towards the industry as a whole.

The incineration of clothes not only makes us question the value of the clothes we buy, it poses a huge environmental question. Doesn't it leave you wondering why the fashion system produces so many garments? This overproduction is all about giving us choice and making the collections enticing. The reality is that there are only a handful of really popular items per collection; sometimes the leftovers get sold in warehouse sales but more often than not it ends up as waste. These companies of course do not want to be destroying their own stock. The problem is created because of the demand to create ever-new styles at an increasing pace and it's the variety within a fashion collection which sells the story of the brand, and the scale which makes it economically viable.

The overproduction of clothing is one of the fashion industry's biggest problems. It also comes at a huge cost in terms of lost revenue and to the environment.

The internet has made it attractive and easy for us to buy our next fashion item. Many of us now prefer to shop online rather than instore. There are so many incentives given to us to buy, and the internet has made it attractive and easy for us to purchase our next fashion item. Many of us now prefer to shop online rather than in stores – with free shipping, discounts and of course the sales, these brands are always working for our attention. Any risk is taken away with the reassuring knowledge that we can click and pay for numerous items and send them back if they aren't right. But have you ever thought about what happens when you do return these items?

A woman I spoke with recently said that she loves the fact she can order a bunch of clothes and just send back the garments she doesn't like. But what appears to be an easy shopping experience comes with a cost. A huge cost. Did you know that most of the fashion returns do not get resold? Instead, it's likely they get marked as waste and are destroyed.

All of this information about industry waste seems like a stark contrast to the idealised images we see online and in magazines of stunning models wearing beautiful clothing. And this is where we are going to need to get real. Of course we love beautiful clothing and want to keep our look new and relevant. But at what cost?

A purchase is not simply an exchange of money for an item. It has so many implications. The large volumes of waste created annually present an issue which is not going away any time soon. Clearly as an industry we've got a lot to do. Change should be driven by the industry, but it will probably be driven by the consumer. Ideally it will be driven by both.

CHAPTER 18

The animal cost

'As a designer I like to work with fabrics that don't bleed.
That's why I avoid all animal skins.'
— Stella McCartney

Animal welfare is not usually the first thing that comes to mind with the fashion industry. When we look at a cashmere jumper in a store, we don't usually think about a herd of goats on a mountain who produced the wool. When we put on our favourite woollen dress or suit it's not likely that we link that clothing to sheep in a paddock. However, when you think about it, a lot of our clothes involve animals in some way or another.

The global animal protection organisation Four Paws released a report in June 2020 which found that only 21% of brands assess even a portion of the animal-derived materials for animal welfare. This means that on the whole the fashion industry is turning a blind eye and animals are suffering as a result.

ANIMALS ARE MADE TO SUFFER FOR OUR FASHION

Globally, over two billion animals are used annually in the wool, fur and leather industries alone (Four Paws). Many of these animals suffer, and are forced to live in unacceptable and substandard conditions. They are subjected to horrendous mutilations, and their lives are filled with fear and terrible stress.

When you dig down into the statistics and stories of what goes on in animal farming it's not pretty, and I'm sure you don't want to read the horror stories here. Hearing about animal cruelty and abuse really disturbs me, as it does many people. It breaks my heart to know that animals are made to suffer for our fashion.

The call for animal rights and more humane treatment has been around for years. More recently it has been gaining significant traction, and the extent to which people were starting to care was made obvious in 2020: the 92nd Academy Awards was made a vegan-themed event. Joaquin Phoenix, an Academy Award Winner, used the event to be a 'voice for the voiceless'. In his speech he said:

> We fear the idea of personal change, because we think we need to sacrifice something; to give something up ... But human beings at our best are so creative and inventive, and we can create, develop and implement systems of change that are beneficial to all sentient beings and the environment.

Ironically, it's all too easy to be removed from the terrible conditions that animals are kept under. I can put my own hand up and say that in the past I haven't thought twice about buying a new leather handbag or pair of shoes, let alone a woollen sweater. But I am now committed to finding alternatives for these products, and I am hesitant to buy anything new. When looking for a new wool sweater, I look on a vintage website or make sure to check that it is from ethical farming practices.

Buying clothing made from animal fur, skins or other products has been a natural way of life for many of us and it really requires a paradigm shift if we are to think of our clothing in a new way. We will still be able to find clothing we love, it will just take more effort to find that next woollen sweater and make sure it comes from small, ethical farming practices or recycled wool that has been turned into something new.

CHAPTER 19

The human cost

'If people starve in the supply chain nothing is sustainable.'
— Simone Cipriani, Ethical Fashion Initiative

There is a juggling act we all need to play when it comes to fashion, especially when finances are involved. But when we buy clothing, do we really consider the true cost that comes as a result of a largely unregulated industry?

All around the world when our clothing is being made, someone somewhere is putting their precious time and energy in. Often the hands that produce our garments come from people in developing countries in conditions that many of us would be appalled at. When you start to dig a little deeper, and not much deeper I can assure you, it all starts to unravel.

In major Western cities around the world, if you were to pay for a blazer to be made locally and from scratch, it would most likely cost more than we are used to paying. All the hours designing and creating the garment would add up. Firstly, there are the many hours to create the pattern and get the shape of the garment right. There are many fittings also. Next there is the handwork required to sew the garment. The type of fabric and machine, the tension and composition of the thread and the skill of the worker all contribute to a beautiful garment. If you request a jacket that has refined craftsmanship there are many hours of sewing involved. This includes finishing the hem, the lining, button closures, and creating elegant invisible seams.

The right environment also contributes. If the craftswoman or craftsman is happy and comfortable where they work, if they are able to take breaks and stretch when needed, it's more likely the garment will be made with attention and care. The cost of the garment would also contribute to a fair wage, as well as the garment worker's sense of purpose and wellbeing in the world. With this fine tailoring, when the person is paid in proportion to the skill and hours they work, it means they can also go home and contribute to their family.

This is an ideal situation. When a person who is sewing a garment in the fashion industry is respected and honoured for their skill. When they are also compensated properly for their time.

THIS IS WHAT'S CURRENTLY HAPPENING IN MANY PARTS OF THE WORLD

There is a misconception that it's just the cheap clothing brands who would be perpetuating this kind of mistreatment. This is actually not the case. Some of the bigger brands, and even the luxury houses, have a long line of incidents around worker neglect in their business. Often they turn a blind eye to these conditions, contracting the work through third parties, although these days there is much more accountability required.

Who has the right to say that someone in a developing country has any less right to a fair wage and working conditions than in Western cities? Part of the problem comes from a lack of legislation and governance in these developing countries. There is also a lack of unions and workers' rights, which leaves fertile ground for abuse and neglect.

This also means that the price of a garment does not necessarily reflect the true cost. Nor are you assured that it was made ethically. No matter how much you could justify it, there is not always a clear correlation between the price we pay and what was involved in the making of a garment. Even with attention to detail, quality of fabrics and good design elements, you always need to dig a little deeper.

On the whole, the fast fashion industry has been the main cause for severe neglect and abuse of human rights in developing countries. By its very nature, fast fashion wants to produce clothing at an increasing rate and speed, and so the garment workers have to work to meet the demand. At the same time, the cost of the clothing is super cheap, which means the workers are on the receiving end with substandard wages.

There is so much disparity from one end of the fashion industry to the other. It takes just four days for a CEO from one of the top five global fashion brands to earn what a Bangladeshi garment worker will earn in their lifetime (Oxfam). It's easy to think of countries such as China and India as where most garment manufacturing takes place. However, the abuse of workers' rights also extends to other countries like Malaysia, Vietnam and Indonesia.

The conditions of these factories are less than ideal, and are often appalling. Neither you nor I would be able to reconcile seeing what actually goes on there. Inside the workplace, the air is toxic and filled with the smell of chemicals from machinery and fabric.

In Bangladesh, 85% of garment workers are women. Earning less than the minimum wage, these women are forced to work excessive hours and somehow manage to get by. But this kind of life comes with another cost, because their salary is not enough to support their children. Wanting to give their children an education and a better life, it's commonplace for these women to send them to live with grandparents or other family members. If you are a parent, I'm sure you would be horrified to have to send your children away at a young age. These women part with their children unwillingly, but the below-average income is often their only option.

On average, women in Bangladesh earn around $3 a day, or approximately $68 a month, all the while being required to work in horrible conditions. This wage is one of the lowest in the world, and is far below the minimum. In research taken up by Oxfam Australia, 72% of workers in Bangladesh and 53% in Vietnam cannot afford healthcare when they are sick. Many of them work overtime without getting paid, and in Vietnam, 75% of workers said that they do not take annual leave so that they can earn extra money.

There is a story of a 23-year-old woman in Bangladesh called Shima. As the leader of the workers' union in her factory, one day she and a group of other women confronted the management requesting better working conditions and fair pay. As a response, these women were taken to a room, locked inside and beaten (The True Cost). These stories are all too common in the garment industry in developing countries.

These workers are often given unrealistic targets for the number of garments they have to sew in a single day. Often they only have one job, like sewing the front and back of a sweater together. Imagine this task on repetition minute after minute, hour after hour. On top of this, they are often reprimanded for falling short of the unrealistic and strict targets given to them. Sometimes they stop taking bathroom and lunch breaks out of fear of what happens when they ask to do so. The contrast in life circumstances between what we expect for ourselves and what they experience could not be more extreme.

If you were to ask a fashion industry professional if much had changed in the rights and conditions of factory workers, I'm sure they would say *no*. The industry overall is still very much guarded about their supply chains. And many deny the fact that they pay their garment workers below the minimum wage. And what is the reason? Profit, of course.

The human cost of the fashion industry is not just isolated to the millions of factory workers. There is also the cost associated with the farmers of crops like cotton, our most popular fibre. In conventional farming, workers are subjected to an array of deadly chemicals, and these farmers have a much shorter life expectancy due to this toxic exposure.

In India, suicide has been growing among cotton farmers. Some people have linked these deaths to expensive genetically modified seeds, as well as the large number of fertilisers and insecticides that are required. Because of increasing costs, farmers turn to loan sharks for extra funds. Under these circumstances, unfortunate weather conditions or a small decrease in the global price of cotton can be fatal.

This chemical problem also extends to leather tanneries. This industry is one of the most toxic in the world. Some of the chemicals involved include chrome, which is linked to cancer. Most of the workers in tanneries suffer from skin pigmentation, severe itching, chronic respiratory problems, skin diseases, and even destruction of the nasal canal. Many workers have died as a result of working in these tanneries.

The chemicals of conventional industries like cotton, leather and other fashion products are just as hazardous for us at home. Just like anything, you can take it at face value or you can find out what's truly involved. If we do not stop and begin to question every purchase we make from now on, it's possible we are contributing to the issue.

In today's world we have become detached from the story behind our clothes. The power of the fashion industry has dehumanised our clothing. The average consumer would not know who made their clothes if asked. Our clothing is usually made by people in countries far away from our daily awareness. Can we continue in this way? I don't think so. I don't want to think that people suffered in order to make my new dress or designer jeans, and I'm sure you don't either.

CHAPTER 20

So what does this all mean?

'Change has to be done now, and done quickly.'
— Sara Maino, *Vogue Italia*

It's very clear there are many systemic and complex issues in the fashion industry. The environment is at a tipping point — business and industry cannot continue to drain the world's resources as they have been. The old model of consumption without consequence is antiquated because the environment is giving us signs that we must slow down.

We have so many reasons to celebrate fashion in this world. It gives us self-expression, it unifies people, it supports livelihoods and economies around the world and it allows for and fosters creativity. However, when you look beneath the surface, it is very clear that there is a world of inequality and abuse taking place. The environment is suffering, natural and finite resources are being used up, and we have a huge waste problem on our hands. In developing countries people feel like the fashion industry gives them a lifeline, whereas in reality it is also threatening their very existence.

It's time to stop the clock and consider what truly matters in this wide world. We do not need lots more clothes on this planet, and the world cannot continue to exist as it has been. It's time for a big reset, where people's lives around the world are taken into account. Where every life is considered equal.

The environment also needs to be taken care of; without it we will cease to exist. If the human race disappeared, the earth would thrive, but while humans continue to take from nature without thinking, our beautiful and precious planet goes more and more out of balance. With this state of imbalance we will be both the cause and the recipients of increasing natural disasters.

Rethinking your fashion means looking at the state of fashion and asking, what is my part in this? How do I feel about what's going on? Do I want to contribute to brands who take no responsibility for their business practices and allow others to suffer? What is my stance on fashion going forward, and what do I want to do about it?

Clearly it is time to rethink our fashion at every level. Rethinking fashion is big, it's complex, it's complicated. But it just has to be done, because there is no alternative.

PART IV

The industry is being called to evolve

'We're all [going to be] using less, spending less. We're going to want to have things that are made to last. I think the new paradigm is that if you're a person or a company and you're in a position to help, you must help. Being sustainable is essential. It is not a choice.'

—Gabriela Hearst

A LOT OF THE TRENDS that have impacted fashion in recent years have come about because of social media, technology and communication. They have given us the ability to communicate and share information freely. It's transformed the planet, and turned it inside out politically and economically. And fashion is the same.

The industry is being called to evolve through a convergence of forces. Some have come about through its own practices, and others are out of its control and happening externally. As traditional structures are being examined, the fashion industry is coming into the limelight. Fashion, which used to be a closed book that would to dictate how we should all look, is now being questioned.

There are many changes taking place in society which are pushing the fashion industry to evolve. These range from wellness to equality and diversity to technology. Fashion exists as a reflection of our values, which are changing. In the coming chapters you will see just how diverse these influences are.

This part is a deeper dive on the industry. It's not just highlighting what needs to change, it's also highlighting the good. It's highlighting the appetite for change. The shift has started, and it's the beginning of a new world. We have more chance of creating change by also focusing on the positives.

CHAPTER 21

Why is the industry being called on to evolve?

'There's a movement for simplifying your life.'
— Yvon Chouinard, Patagonia

We are at a point in time where a convergence of events is calling the fashion industry to evolve. Technology, the availability of information and an escalating environmental catastrophe are changing the way people perceive fashion. This means they are asking for it to adjust its outdated models to meet the needs of today.

The fashion industry can no longer exist as it has been. Years ago it was a closed book. We took everything at face value, and would be ready to hear about the latest trends at a moment's notice. We stood by to learn how to dress and what to buy. There was no questioning. Then along came a world of interconnection and social media, and everything began to change. As people started to share information, we became aware of what really goes on behind the scenes. We started to question the true cost of a garment. We became aware of issues that may have been there for many years but were only increasing with the rise of fast fashion. Things like waste and its damage to the environment, as well as the humanitarian impact. As we heard these stories around the world, it became obvious that the glossy image of the industry was just one aspect of the whole.

IT'S A BRAVE NEW WORLD

Technology has enabled people to share information and question social systems and structures in their own way. The power of choice really has been handed back to the individual, and with this people are starting to demand transparency, accountability and authenticity. As people have started to share the truth about themselves and the things they believe in, it has brought about a change in values. While we once saw success as a shiny new object or a status or a position, this has all begun to change.

Fashion, which was based on the aspirational, now has to align to a new set of values. These new values are demanding that the industry adjust and becomes more inclusive. That a fashion brand acts responsibly and as a part of society, not as something that dictates how we should look and feel.

People now also want the brands they buy from to be socially and environmentally conscious. We are all so aware of climate change. We can't ignore it, and it's becoming very obvious that the fashion industry, one of the most resource-intensive industries in the world, has a *huge* role to play.

Values are changing, as you will read more about in the next chapter, and this is a massive driver behind the call for accountability and transparency. The needs of today require everyone to step up and contribute to greater equality and greater acceptance. The impact of the industry on the environment is real, and it's time for a radical transformation of fashion's contribution to all of these issues.

CHAPTER 22

We're living in a world of changing values

'Demand quality, not only in the products you buy, but in the lives of the people who made it.' — Orsola de Castro

Our values are influenced by so many factors, and what we value changes over time. Our values are influenced by life experience, our environment, and how much knowledge we have to make informed decisions at any point in our life.

WE ARE MORE INFORMED THAN EVER

The explosion of technology and information has meant we are more informed than ever. We can find answers to almost any question either by searching online or reaching out to our virtual networks and asking. We are more informed about our local environment, as well as global issues. We are also more aware of ourselves; by sharing information we get to assess how we truly feel and what we truly need, and that in itself brings change.

We now have so much information and knowledge that it has become like a call for personal and global evolution. It has brought personal empowerment on so many levels. It's never been easier to start a business, grow a community of followers or create a movement. Think of the #MeToo movement, which exposed such terrible abuse and disempowerment. The strength of this movement is largely the result of social media, magnifying the ability to expose inequality and bring it to the light. Women's rights were brought to the fore on a whole new level. Many companies saw that they had to act and get on board or they too may be accused of the same.

The Covid-19 pandemic has also changed the world and the fashion industry. Giorgio Armani recently commented on this in an interview with the *Financial Review* in Australia:

> We are now beginning to understand what true luxury is: the freedom to walk outside, to travel, to see our friends and loved ones. In this context we may well have a different attitude to luxury goods. We may appreciate the simple things in life more, and so when we come to purchase items, we may well do so more thoughtfully, with more consideration, and appreciate them all the more for it.

The pandemic brought the fashion industry to its knees in so many ways, and it will never be the same again. It also brought to light many systemic issues. There have been many conversations in industry publications and interviews recognising that it was time for the industry to rethink the way it has been doing things. Even Anna Wintour, the editor of *Vogue* US, spoke about this on Naomi Campbell's YouTube talk show *No Filter with Naomi*. She said:

> I think it is an opportunity for all of us to look at our industry and look at our lives and rethink our values, and to really think about the waste and amount of money and consumption and excess, and I obviously include myself in this, that we've all indulged in, and we really need to rethink what this industry stands for.

This shows us that values are also changing within the industry. It's easy to wave a big stick and say the industry has to change, but the reality is that the industry also *wants* to change. That's because the people within it want a future for their own industry. They also want change for themselves because they don't want to work in the same way any more. They also want a future for their children and the health of the planet.

Acknowledgements like this by industry leaders show that values truly are changing for all. Whether we are ready or not, we know that change must happen. This I believe is influencing us to act, and will be the driving force of the industry today and into the future.

CHAPTER 23

The global sustainability movement is here to stay

'It's a mindset, a culture, a lifestyle, and one that is accessible to all.' — Amy Powney

Recognition by fashion industry leaders that it's time for change makes it evident that the conversation is finally cutting through. Sustainability, a topic that was once alternative, has now gone mainstream. It has left the sidelines and positioned itself on centre court.

IT'S TIME

One of the indicators that sustainability is being taken seriously is that we are more environmentally conscious than ever. Many cities around the world are banning the use of plastic bags. Companies are phasing out single-use plastic. With prices dropping, and governments offering incentives, solar panels are becoming more accessible then ever to install.

Environmental issues are at the front of our awareness, and there are people stepping forward to lead the way. Greta Thunberg is one of these inspired hearts. Her young, passionate voice definitely struck a chord around the world. She ignited a global movement and inspired strikes in major cities and smaller towns. She resonated in a way that no other person has been able to. And why? Because she speaks with moral authority and cuts to our hearts because she is the next generation and will have to live through the impact of climate change. 'You have stolen my dreams and my childhood with your empty words,' Thunberg said at the United Nations General Assembly in 2019.

We also stood up and took notice because, globally, culturally and socially we have been having this conversation in various forms for many years. We were ready to hear. It's time. The belief that we need to act has set in. We have accepted that we all have a responsibility if we want change and a future on this planet.

Within fashion itself, young designers have been driving the shift towards sustainability, approaching fashion in new ways and being willing to adopt innovative approaches. One of these is zero-waste design. A lot of textile waste in the industry is caused simply through cutting out pattern pieces from fabric. The aim of zero-waste design is to use fabric in a way where nothing is left over as scraps or sent to waste.

More and more fashion brands, big and small, are getting on board. Some of these are reusing fabrics from previous collections (which are usually sent to waste). Other brands are converting to organic cotton or switching to processes that reduce chemical use. And some designers are creating clothing by repurposing old clothing and refashioning it into completely new garments. While a lot of the industry remains silent on the sustainability issue, it's the brands who are standing up for change who are showing the rest of the industry that it is possible. In this way, I anticipate there will be more and more businesses getting on board.

CHAPTER 24

A new model:
the circular economy

'Can things change quickly? Absolutely. History has shown us that. What we need is a *direction.*' — Ellen MacArthur

A ROBUST AND COMPLETELY NEW SOLUTION

One of the biggest influences driving fashion towards a better future is a model called a 'circular economy'. If the industry is going to change, it needs to transform completely, and there is no time to waste.

A circular model proposes a robust and completely new solution. This new model is being led by the Ellen MacArthur Foundation. Dame Ellen MacArthur was raised in Derbyshire, UK, and made history in 2005 by becoming the fastest person to sail solo around the world without stopping, in just over 70 days. During her time sailing, with limited resources on board to survive the trip, she became very aware of what finite resources really were. She understood in parallel that we only have finite resources on this planet, and they are being used at a rate we cannot sustain.

After retiring from professional sailing in 2010, she launched the Ellen MacArthur Foundation, a charity that focuses on a transition to a circular economy. Since its inception, the charity has become a global thought leader. Decision-makers across business, government and academia have taken this into their agenda.

A circular economy is based on three principles:

- designing out waste and pollution

- keeping products and materials in use

- regenerating natural systems.

A circular economy works to ensure that once a product has been created, it is kept in use for as long as possible. When a product wears out or comes to the end of its life, a circular economy aims to recycle these products back into raw materials, and have them remade into products once again. This process is – as the name implies – circular, recycling and recreating clothing over and again.

This model decreases the use of new materials to make garments, which is a benefit to the environment, the earth's atmosphere and the future of our planet. It also increases the use of already existing materials, and this means that an incredible amount of value is released and created. This new model can save companies millions of dollars.

In the current model, most fashion businesses take from natural resources, make a product, and the clothing is then discarded at the end of its life – there is no real plan for what happens after a product is purchased by a consumer. There is a huge amount of textile waste created, and an even greater amount of money is wasted. Today the industry relies on 98 million tonnes of non-renewable resources including oil to produce our clothing every year (Ellen MacArthur Foundation). These precious resources and the fabrics our clothing are made of, are discarded without thinking about utilising them further. It is estimated that this is a loss of around US$500 billion of value every year (Ellen MacArthur Foundation).

So imagine, with a circular economy the fashion industry can work to turn these discarded resources into profitable ones. That is US$500 billion of value waiting to be utilised. It also means an incredible amount of resources would not be extracted, harvested or depleted from the environment because the old ones are being repurposed.

In a report by the Ellen MacArthur Foundation titled 'A New Textiles Economy', it is stated that there are four areas or ambitions for this new vision. They are:

1. To phase out substances of concern as well as toxic microfibre release into the oceans. This means phasing out chemical use, which includes decreasing the creation of manmade fabrics – such as polyester – that come from petroleum.

2. To increase the use of clothing.

3. To radically improve and increase recycling.

4. To effectively use resources and move to renewable materials like sustainably sourced fibres. It would also mean reducing water usage, being more energy efficient and reducing the use of fossil fuels and chemicals.

While a circular textile economy is still in its early days, many brands are taking these principles on board and finding ways to incorporate them. A circular economy is not a panacea, however it does show us that there are other ways for the industry to operate. It also provides a truly compelling roadmap for action.

CHAPTER 25

Lifestyles are changing

'Modern life requires us to be more and more flexible in our attire.' — Giorgio Armani

The day I realised that casual clothing had taken hold was when people started wearing sneakers to the haute couture runways in Paris. Standing outside the Dior show at the Musée Rodin on the Left Bank, fashion bloggers were snapping their cameras everywhere. Bloggers had been the new fashion paparazzi-slash-journalists in the industry for some time, but the new normal was to wear pimped out, pumped up, glamourised, or just plain white street shoes.

We had all seen this evolution coming — remember athleisure? The craze which had people suddenly wearing their workout gear to the supermarket with no intention of going to the gym? This trend hasn't gone anywhere; it will continue to evolve. It's a sign that people are looking for more utilitarian and relaxed clothing that works for them.

'CLOTHES THAT WORK AS HARD AS I DO'

The explosion of casual clothing has been on the upswing for some time now, and it is representative of our connected and plugged in, globalised world. Technology has made communication efficient and mobile, meaning we can do a work meeting from home then rush off to take the kids to school while stopping for a beauty treatment on the way home. Our professional lives are no longer divided with a clear line of going to the office and then coming home after a standard workday.

This change in our routines means our needs are also changing. We need clothes that can do more, more often. In the words of Suzy Menkes, a respected fashion critic, 'clothes that work as hard as I do'.

Many of us have more autonomy in our lives than ever before. We have a greater ability to build a business from scratch in a relatively short amount of time. We can also sell our services and products in a way that suits us, and the way we work has become more about the value we bring than the company or people we work for. There is a lot of leverage, and this choice means we also have more choice with what we wear.

Even in the office environment around the world we have seen dress codes become more relaxed. Men, when was the last time you wore a tie? I'm sure you are not wearing one as often as you were years ago. As Arianna Huffington said:

> The culture of work is changing, and with it, our office dress codes. Companies are encouraging staffers to bring their whole selves to work — and people are embracing style repeats and 'personal uniforms' in an effort to de-stress workwear.

This focus on bringing our whole selves to work has been happening in the office as well as personal businesses. You may have become immune to the word 'authenticity' since it reached peak use in the last few years. Modern authenticity is the result of our technological age, and the more we share information, the more room there will be to play life to our own tune.

So, what does this mean for fashion? It means clothing has become more and more functional and we need less variety in clothing. We want our outfits to be effortless so that we can move about life with ease. Dressing up is more of a rarity, and if anything, clothing has become more about going from home to the office to dinner, all in the same outfit. Not that I necessarily agree with the departure of dressing our best and opting for casual, because personally I like to be more dressed up, but I do think there is a beneficial element to this movement.

More than just clothes, there is a greater call for us to be genuine. To turn up as our real selves; this has turned the focus away from consumerism. Even today as I write this chapter I read a quote from Alessandro Michele, the head designer for Gucci, who has decided that the brand will no longer be showing and creating clothes to the traditional schedule. Gucci is stepping away from the unrealistic pace of the fashion industry, opting for fewer shows per year. Alessandro said in an interview, 'I need time to be more real and more caring'. In the same way, each of us has greater ability to live life to our own tune and it is being shown in our choices of more relaxed and more wearable, versatile and functional clothing.

CHAPTER 26

Fashion and wellbeing

'Delete the negative; accentuate the positive.' — Donna Karan

So where has the focus moved to if we're not thinking as much about our next fashion purchase? Wellbeing. Yes, that's right. So when I say that lifestyles are changing, the focus has really moved towards lifestyle itself. We want quality of life, and this may mean working fewer hours or going to the gym. Each of us has in some way been influenced by the lifestyle and wellbeing trend.

I would even say this is less of a trend and more of a movement. We are working to become more aware in every area of our lives. The words 'conscious' and 'ethical' are popping up not only in marketing messages but as a grassroots movement. People are sharing information freely on how they are improving their lives, and it is becoming the norm. A culture of wellbeing has arrived.

FASHION IS NOW PART OF A BIGGER PICTURE

Have you ever taken a yoga class? You would be in the minority if you said you hadn't. Just follow someone walking down the road wearing high-fashion leggings with a mat under their arm and they will take you to the door of a yoga studio.

Or maybe a personal trainer is more your style? Years ago having a personal trainer was for the elite. Now, it's a recommended activity. Personal trainers have grown as a profession. The benefits of daily activity are shared widely across social media. On a morning or evening walk you can see training groups moving in rhythm and sharing each other's company.

Over the last 10 years as the blogosphere has taken off, we have seen the growth of 'lifestyle' sites. They cover everything from feeling good to looking good. You will find a smoothie recipe along with a link to the latest activewear to jump into as you pulse your greens and run to a yoga class. The best sites are not a marketing ploy, they are a business based on experience. A desire to share the benefits of their own wellness practices and personal growth.

I remember when I moved to India to study meditation in 1998; it was a very alternative thing to do. Could many people understand it? Probably not, but now its time has come. The uptake of meditation has been increasing for many years. This beneficial practice has been endorsed by Oprah, Seinfeld and many other celebrities – not to say that this an indicator of its relevance but more so that when they are talking about it, there must be an audience ready to hear. Meditation apps are some of the most popular on our phones.

When we talk about meditation, mindfulness also rings in the air. It has become an overly saturated term in recent years, and the lines have blurred between the two. I am a purest and believe that meditation and mindfulness are completely different things. Either way, the fact that they both are trending is significant. Globally, people are wanting personal transformation and are taking up these practices in huge numbers.

You can attend meditation retreats in places like Bali, or perhaps instead a wellness retreat. Or a detox. In the '80s, wellness went mainstream and retreats were the latest big thing with celebrities. Fast forward to today and this experiential health trend is accessible to just about everybody.

The uptake of wellness and lifestyle activities shows that optimal health and self-development are now aspirational. Deepening our sense of calm and wellbeing are the new benchmarks of a good life, and they are taking hold of us all. Fashion is now part of a greater outlook on life. People still want to look good, but most of all they want to *feel* good.

Fashion still has a big role to play in this, but it's a very different role compared to even just a few years ago. This wellbeing trend shows us that as we become more conscious and more aware, we want to see this reflected in life overall, in not only the food we buy and exercise we engage in but also the clothes we buy. This wellbeing trend also fits in with the growing movement for business to be ethical and sustainable. It's all to do with a movement for the greater good.

CHAPTER 27

The 'all bodies' movement and inclusivity

'Personality begins where comparison ends.'
— Karl Lagerfeld

Walking into a fashion boutique looking for an item you need is not as straight forward as you might think. To begin with, sizes usually only range from a 0 to 14 or 16, or for men up to an XXL at the best of times. But then even if you find a pair of pants in the right size, it doesn't mean they will fit you properly. Each of us has a unique body shape and size, some wider in the waist and others in the hips. It's unrealistic to think there is a one-size-fits-many in this diverse world. And yet for the most part the fashion industry caters to a select group.

For so long the world of fashion has had a very definite type of woman on the runway and in magazines. We know her far too well. She is easy to spot, skinny, often almost emaciated, and tall with perfect features and flawless skin. But there is a new emerging silhouette, and she is not just one size. It has taken time, and for a while it seemed more like a token gesture of a brand rather than a genuine effort. It has been a tough cookie to break, understandably when the entire industry is based on one ideal of beauty.

We are at an all-time high of size inclusivity. This new silhouette is not just one size; it is the silhouette of the real woman or man.

THE SIZE INCLUSIVE MOVEMENT

The size inclusive movement started in the US in the '60s, as a way to raise awareness about the barriers faced by obese people. Since then, social acceptance of being overweight has had a slow but steady trajectory. In recent years the body positive movement has been very loud. While a giant step in the right direction, it has been somewhat tarnished and gentrified with highly photogenic plus-size models taking the limelight, as well as an ongoing size limit on what is actually considered acceptable in marketing material.

In terms of size inclusivity, we are not talking about health here, or the size at which a person becomes unhealthy, which is also an individual measure. The topic of a healthy weight is a different issue. We are talking about the current turning of the tide against the power of fashion media and brands to portray an unrealistic standard of beauty. It is ridiculous to even have to say that whatever your body shape you are worthy and beautiful, but unfortunately fashion media has a big influence on our perception of ourselves.

Again, technology has turned the standard model (get it?) of beauty upside down. People are able to share themselves authentically and unashamedly on Instagram and other channels. The most audacious ones are gathering a huge following, which is breaking down social barriers one influencer at a time.

A significant moment for the industry was in 2015 when the French Government passed a law that banned obsessively thin models on the runway. It was a step in the right direction, and since then, slowly but surely we have seen more shapes and sizes as well as ages walking the catwalk. And why is this significant? Because it's industry bodies and the brands who employ the models who have such influence on society and its perception of normal.

Fashion media is now coming on board, and we are seeing new standards of beauty arising on the front pages of magazines, pushing for greater acceptance overall, with people like Winnie Harlow, a Canadian fashion model and public spokesperson on the skin condition vitiligo, or Andreja Pejić, a Bosnian-Australian transgender model. She broke new ground in fashion after starting as a male and going on to become a hugely successful androgynous runway model on the international scene.

As I write this I'm also reflecting on the past few months where the Black Lives Matter movement has been at the front and centre of our lives. After George Floyd's life was cut short by a policeman for no reason at all, the world was talking about white privilege and the divide of inequality. This conversation extended to the fashion industry, where brands were condemned if they didn't get on board. Not declaring a position on the matter was considered as another voice towards inequality.

On Instagram we started seeing live conversations with black leaders; people were diving deep and exploring the issue so we could truly understand what it all meant. Magazines took a stance and started using black models on the cover, as did fashion brands on the release of their new collections. There were conversations in industry publications about why we weren't already using more black models on the runway and why we didn't have more black leaders.

The fashion industry was put under the spotlight, and for good reason. The big publishing houses witnessed staff standing down with allegations of racism which came out into the open. The Black Lives Matter movement in fashion is another example of the way diversity and equality that have needed to be addressed for a long time.

The longest running British *Vogue* editor Alexandra Shulman was a trailblazer in fashion media for a movement towards inclusivity. She began persuading fashion designers to move away from the ultra-skinny look and instead use 'real' women on the runway. Alexandra also made a bold and brave statement with an Instagram post on her personal account in 2017 when at 59 years of age she posed unashamedly with all her lumps and bumps in a bikini. This strong message was understood as a statement to help normalise body shapes and inspire greater inclusivity.

As you can see, the 'standard' type of beauty is being challenged and forced to evolve. Acceptance and authenticity are at the heart of this movement. This positive stance goes a long way towards the way we think about fashion. It's prompting us to rethink what beauty truly means, to accept ourselves, and it demands a greater respect for all.

CHAPTER 28

Community and collaboration

'Society is now about exchange and the new economy
and working together in teams and groups.'
— Li Edelkoort

The power of community is also changing fashion. By going online and sharing beliefs and interests, people are building their own communities. They are creating new styles, mixing genres of clothing and breaking down stereotypes of how we are meant to look and feel. Through online groups people get to feel that they are a part of something bigger than themselves. The strength of a community can start a movement, and it can also facilitate personal change.

We all know about influencers, and while some of us might not agree with the highly curated and photoshopped world some of them display, it does show the power of individual people to build their own following and personal brands. This has been a huge disruptor for fashion, but it has also been an asset. If there is an authentic alignment between a fashion brand and an influencer it can truly elevate the message they are trying to share. I'm not really a fan of influencers when it isn't built on substance or a deeper message. However, if you think about those who are doing good in the world they also are harnessing the use of social platforms to generate change. And this is where they access the power of a community to get behind their cause.

Building a community through shared beliefs is transforming the way we go about our lives and putting the focus on a greater good.

A movement can simply be a group of passionate people sharing a hobby, or it can be sharing a cause that many people resonate with. This is evident with Facebook groups — I'm sure you're part of at least one or two. In the fashion realm, communities have started around swapping clothes and reselling pieces from popular brands that still hold a lot of value even when secondhand. Sometimes really coveted pieces will sell in seconds for higher than the original price.

ARE CLOTHING RENTALS THE WAY OF THE FUTURE?

There is also the sharing economy, which harnesses the power of community. Rather than buy clothing, why not share through rental? You can now access high-end designer pieces to wear for an event and then take them back for someone else to enjoy. There is a lot of talk in fashion about rental being the future. The movement is growing, and as more people become comfortable with wearing clothes that someone else has used, it will truly take hold. With sustainability the issue of our times, it is one of the best solutions to the volume of clothes that are already circulating the planet.

With rental, you can find a statement piece that is appropriate for the occasion and use it to highlight your already existing and fabulously curated wardrobe. Imagine you have a business dinner where you need to present professionally but would like to improve your style. Why not rent a Balmain or Saint Laurent blazer and add that extra touch of luxury to your outfit?

Community and collaboration are also key to the future of fashion; we are seeing people of all industries come together to find solutions to the issues of waste and diminishing resources. For example, a designer may collaborate with a textile developer, startups from Silicon Valley and biochemical engineers to come up with new sustainable products and solutions. Collaborations like this are happening frequently and are a way to bring fresh eyes to the issues facing the fashion industry.

CHAPTER 29

Brands with a conscience

'To do good, you actually have to do something.'
— Yvon Chouinard, Patagonia

Increasingly it is being shown that people are consciously choosing to support brands who care about more than just their product. Millennials have been driving this trend, and yet on the whole, people of all ages and backgrounds are demanding more. They are asking that brands adapt and commit themselves to giving back to society through a greater cause than their own.

While there are many companies that are adapting and evolving to the changing expectations and needs of their customers and the world as a whole, there are some that have had an extraordinary culture from the very beginning. This is long before social media was a thing, and back when the environment was simply seen as a resource.

A COMPANY ABSOLUTELY COMMITTED TO DOING THE RIGHT THING

Before Yvon Chouinard founded the company Patagonia, he was a blacksmith, forging climbing equipment for local climbers in California. He made things called 'pitons' in a small forge in his parents' backyard. He made his pitons and then travelled around California, selling them from the back of his car. This was really a lifestyle business that enabled the young Chouinard to travel, to surf and to rock climb.

As climbing was a growing sport, demand for his pitons grew and he became busier. Chouinard built a small team to keep up with the demand, and by 1970 they had become the largest supplier of climbing hardware. The company Patagonia was formed in 1973. But he also started to notice something not so good. With all of the extra rock climbing going on, and the nature of how they climbed, damage was being done to the rock walls by the equipment that was hammered into them being left behind and breaking sheets of rock. He realised that they were destroying the thing they had come to enjoy, and he knew that something had to be done.

Chouinard developed new climbing equipment that was far more environmentally friendly and less damaging to the rock walls. This was revolutionary. His company Chouinard Equipment started manufacturing the new, more environmentally responsible equipment and straight away the new products became incredibly successful.

In a logical business evolution, Chouinard realised that there was demand for other products and services from his climbers, things like jumpers, beanies, gloves and boots. But the more the business started to look around for products to sell, the more they realised the gaps in the materials being used and the limited application of what already existed. And that was an opportunity on many levels.

To cut a long story short (and it is definitely worth reading Chouinard's autobiography *Let My People Go Surfing* to get the full picture), Patagonia was formed and it became a company built on finding better solutions for the needs of their customers. And by better, it wanted not only better clothing for climbing and other outdoor pursuits, but also clothing made from more sustainable and environmentally friendly materials, made with processes and systems that were ethically and socially responsible, long before many of these conversations were being had more widely. They held themselves to the highest standards – and they knew that they could keep getting better.

If you scan through the Patagonia site it becomes very clear, very quickly that this is a company absolutely committed to doing the right thing. In fact, there are so many revolutionary things they have done over close to 50 years that when you look at the company today, it is without a doubt a role model for the future.

Patagonia is also a certified B Corp company. This is one of the highest and strictest certifications for a business that solves social and environmental problems. The former CEO of Patagonia Rose Marcario has said:

> The B Corp movement is one of the most important of our lifetime, built on the simple fact that business impacts and serves more than just shareholders — it has an equal responsibility to the community and to the planet.

This is a company driven by a truly responsible culture, started by the founder, shared by the employees. Every single aspect of the business is under scrutiny to do better, to be responsible, to play a role, to not accept the status quo. And a few short paragraphs here cannot do justice to the sheer extent of how this company continually raises the bar environmentally, socially, ethically and financially. This is a company that has a big picture purpose, a strong sense of identity and responsibility, and model of transparency that is inspiration on many levels.

CHAPTER 30

Transparency and accountability

'There are those that say we shouldn't put too much emphasis on transparency, after all, it is self-declared. But for me, it may not necessarily lead to best practice, but it does lead to a culture of scrutiny and vigilance, and is that first step to understanding the industry and the supply chain.' — Orsola de Castro

As we saw with the Patagonia example, some brands are honest and transparent about their practices to the core. This kind of transparency really is a powerful model for all fashion brands if they want to be relevant in the future. Transparency is the catalyst for greater improvement. It engenders accountability. It creates trust, and it defines the culture of a brand.

While there is a lot of talk around transparency, what we are truly looking for is *change*. The fashion transparency index released in 2020 by Fashion Revolution states:

Transparency is a tool for change, not the end goal. Transparency is not a silver bullet that will solve the many complex and deeply systemic problems in the global fashion industry. However, transparency provides a window into the conditions in which our clothes are being made and allows us to address them more quickly and collaboratively.

As we can see by this statement, being transparent about how a business runs behind closed doors is the first step to change. It requires a commitment to improve in the future. Once a business or a company opens up those doors and provides a window into its supply chain and practices, the next step that comes with it is accountability. You can't just be transparent and do nothing about it. Transparency requires new objectives and new targets.

WHICH WOULD YOU CHOOSE?

The one thing that will help us as customers make more informed decisions is when we have enough information about what went into making a garment, and this only comes about through transparency. If I was to hold up two seemingly identical pairs of jeans with the same wash, cut and stitching and one was $150 and the other $29.99, which would you choose? Would you take a breath and ask yourself why one is so cheap and the other five times the price? What would be the reason for you to choose the more expensive pair when you could save so much money?

The first obvious answer I would expect is that the more expensive pair was better quality. And I would congratulate you if quality was one of the main drivers behind your fashion purchases. However, cost is not always representative of quality, and this is why we need to dig a little deeper. There is much more to consider. The real difference is when you look into the supply chain of the fashion brand itself. It's the details that tell us whether or not a garment was sourced and created sustainably and made ethically.

It's most likely that there are real implications involved with a product if it's sold below a certain price point. A product can only be cheap when it is made at a huge scale which means the cost per garment is lower. An extremely cheap price usually means labour conditions are compromised and the clothing is made in unethical factories where workers rights are not respected.

A cheaper price is also reflected in the quality of the fabric. This often means the fabric is synthetic or made of a very low grade natural fibre, like a poor-quality cotton for example. If it's a low-grade natural fibre then the processes used to make that fabric are also compromised. Toxic chemicals are often used to treat these fabrics. From growing or making the fibre to dyeing the fabrics, right through to treatment processes that make sure your jeans don't shrink when you receive them and that they look good on the hanger. Because it's all about hanger appeal instore, right?

Once you pay for the product and get it home, the cheaper product is most likely going to wear out quickly, shrink or go out of shape. This causes another problem, which is waste. When the average person is dissatisfied with a garment they either throw it away or send it back to the store. Unfortunately, it's likely that the company is only going to incinerate it or send it to landfill.

Knowing this, what would your choice be now? Can you see that before we can make informed decisions we need all the information? We need complete transparency from fashion brands. We need to know exactly what type of cotton was used, and whether it was organic or sourced from farms that use minimal chemicals. We need to know the quality of that cotton, and then where it was made and how robust and committed to quality a factory is when they turn that cotton into fabric. The list goes on, because all along the supply chain each process matters.

Most of us not only want, we demand transparency. In society today, millennials and gen Z are placing a lot of focus on brands and demanding social and environmental responsibility. And yet, with all these demands, a majority of fashion brands fail to acknowledge or care about disclosing their practices. Many brands turn away from recognising that their business practices could be contributing to environmental damage and human neglect within the supply chain.

When we talk about transparency, we are not just talking about boasting of an organic range of t-shirts. Transparency is about showing customers how all of their products are created and in what conditions. It's about disclosing all the practices that may or may not impact on the planet, people and the product itself.

Before now, the entire fashion system has put profits before the well-being of the environment and people. The truth is that at some point there has to be a limit. We simply cannot allow brands to create or act in this way anymore. Individually, this means you and I need to demand disclosure about all the processes and people involved in the supply chain of our favourite brands.

CHAPTER 31

The ever-increasing impact of social media

'Thanks to social media, there are very few secrets.'
— Carment Busquets

Technology has changed the way we live and communicate. A big part of this is due to social media and global connectivity. Social media has brought people power, it has toppled governments, and started movements that have raised our awareness of an issue to a whole new level.

Since social media took hold, each one of us has had the ability to share what we know to be true and reach the people who need to hear it. We are able to have a voice on issues we feel passionate about and have the ability to reach people of influence who can help our cause. If our message resonates on a deep level, it may go viral. Thousands and millions of people can get involved at the click of a button. Social media has given rise to greater equality and transparency. And while you may have seen the documentary *The Social Dilemma* which examines the complexities behind access to our data, at the same time social media has also been a catalyst for good. It has broken down barriers and allowed for greater accessibility to information.

Fashion, which was once a tightly held industry, has seen its power shift within the past two decades. Imagine a fashion show in Paris which used to be exclusive and coveted; it was only accessible to fashion journalists, wealthy buyers and industry heavyweights. As bloggers and influencers came on the scene, you could find a young woman with many thousands of followers but no professional experience within the industry being given a seat in the row behind some of the top fashion editors. When it started happening there was a huge outrage, but brands and industry leaders had to adapt because it was becoming the new normal.

So what is the benefit of this vast ocean of information? We now have more power to make up our own minds than ever before. We can research an issue or product from all angles and come to our own decision. We can chase down the source of that information and ask more questions. There is no end to our ability to learn, and grow.

The fashion industry has been shifting, shaping and adapting to this virtual world. Years ago there was less opportunity to learn, read and share about fashion. Magazines were the main outlet, and we had limited places to buy our clothes. Since social media and ecommerce came into being, fashion has become more democratised.

THERE IS NOWHERE TO HIDE

The power of social media and its impact on the fashion industry was never more apparent than when the garment factory Rana Plaza collapsed in Bangladesh in 2013. When it happened, knowledge of this event was not isolated to India and within the fashion industry. The greater global community found out immediately. News of this pivotal and horrific event was being shared on cell phones, in pictures, through Facebook, email and Twitter – the news was everywhere.

More and more people are now looking to find out what really happens when a garment is created. They also want to know just how much abuse of human rights exists for the poorest of the poor, those who make our clothes day by day and receive little in return. Social media and transparency truly go hand in hand.

We now know much about what is truly taking place in the fashion industry. Social media has been the great democratiser. As brands try to promote aspirational products, new communities and individuals stand up and take a position to show us that it doesn't matter what you look like or who you are, you have a place in this world. The new aspirational identity is one that is free. One that is able to express themselves and be accepted just as they are.

Even though there is so much fake and highly curated content on the internet, there is also a lot of authenticity and truth telling. People are busting myths like the ideal body or the ideal life. Human values of inclusivity, kindness and compassion are being explored, valued and promoted just as much as the new 'it' handbag.

As we go forward we can harness the power of social media to find out the true value of any product or brand the we are interested in. What is the social stance? What is the tone of their messaging? All this is visible at the next click or swipe of our screen. And all of this is only going to increase, so for a fashion brand there really is nowhere to hide.

CHAPTER 32

Increasingly we want to know about the people behind the brand

'Who makes it, who benefits from it, how many lives can a garment sustain?' — Rahul Mishra

More and more we want to know where our garments are made, by whom, and if this gives back to a culture and a community. We want to feel that our purchases matter. We want stories and information that help us connect and engage with the products and the brand.

It's now not enough for a business to just talk about their product and how it will enhance someone's life. These days there are so many clothes available, but what is their real value? Do they have a story that matters? The vast majority of clothing is pumped out in factories without much thought or meaning. For big brands, clothing is a commodity. It doesn't matter to them what farm that cotton came from or how it was made; it's just about numbers.

This kind of thoughtless product is very different from what people actually want. Many people want to know not just about the brand but the people behind the brand. Every small detail is appreciated.

CONNECTING WITH THE PROCESS

One brand that has always shown incredible attention to detail is the luxury brand Hermès. I truly came to understand this when I attended their pop-up exhibition called Hermès At Work in Melbourne. It was held in a beautiful historical building, and the purpose of the exhibition was to give people an insight into how some of their most iconic products are made.

The exhibition was displayed in a circular form around a large room decorated with 10 individual work stations. Each of these display areas was set up so that you could see their products being created in real life. Hermès had brought out a group of artisans from France who each specialised in a unique craft. One by one they told us about their artisanal work and the craftsmanship that goes into making Hermès ties, scarves, bags, gloves, saddles, jewellery and more.

One woman in particular truly stood out to me. She told us she had been working as a tie maker for Hermès for many years and had created thousands of ties in her time there. She spoke about the stitching at the back of a tie, and how it needs to be loose so that the tie will sit nicely when it is worn. She said if the stitching is too tight then it doesn't sit properly. This woman also mentioned that each tie can be traced back to its maker and identified by their signature handwork.

This initiative was a wonderful way of connecting us to the value of a single handcrafted item. Learning from these artisans gave an insight into the true value of a single tie, a pair of gloves or an iconic Hermès scarf. Hearing from this woman gave me an emotional connection with the brand in a way that I didn't have before. It also reminded me of the value, beauty, longevity and quality of a handmade garment or accessory. This experience goes to show just how much of a difference it makes to know the story behind a product and a brand.

There is another brand I came across recently, a small business that does all their design and production under the one building. The thing that impressed me the most is that on their website when you look at any product you can find out the intricate details of how it was made, right down to the name of the person who made it.

This kind of connection to the people and the process can be given by any brand that cares about the individuals who make their products and how they are made. When you think about any beautiful textile or garment that is worthwhile you can trace it back to a person, a place and a process and this is where true value lies.

PART V

We can make a difference

'We can heal our planet with our power as consumers.'

—Carment Busquets

NOW, MORE THAN EVER, we have the ability to effect positive change in the fashion industry. We can also make positive changes to our own wardrobes. We can restructure our personal fashion collections so that we want to wear more of what's inside. So that our clothes inspire and empower us whenever we put on an outfit. And so that each piece of clothing we own reflects a personal move towards better buying decisions. Change comes through awareness. It comes through an appreciation of what each purchase actually means.

Change takes place personally as well as socially. It can come about through sharing information. We can exchange views with other people and start a conversation that will influence others to make better buying decisions. We can also go online and search for the information we seek, and then act accordingly. If we want to find out about a particular brand and learn about their supply chains or who makes their clothes, we can. And then, if we don't find any information that also tells us a great deal. Either way, our search for information is at our fingertips. And this in turn empowers us to make decisions. Each piece of information counts. Every action counts. All in the move towards a better future.

CHAPTER 33

Just because it's sustainable doesn't mean it can't be beautiful

'Beauty is a form of activism.' — Li Edelkoort

If the clothing we buy and wear is not appealing or aesthetically pleasing, what's the point? In the past there have been myriad associations around sustainable fashion. Visions of hemp clothing, shapeless linen kaftans, and the belief that sustainable fashion is basically craft, sometimes not being made well. So much has changed, and you can now truly find stunning pieces with a conscience.

The term 'sustainable fashion' has had a reinvention, just as this book proposes we need to rethink our fashion. To be sustainable is a way of life and a way of thinking about how we do things. It's not bound to a certain style or type of craft. And at the same time, if you're looking for beautiful classic pieces then there are many designers you will find these from. Designers like Stella McCartney and Gabriella Hearst are committed to beautiful products with design integrity that are also sustainable. Stella McCartney says:

> First and foremost I'm a fashion designer. I've studied to be a fashion designer and I believe in luxury, I believe in beauty, I believe in desirability. I think there is this kind of thought process when it comes to sustainable fashion that you're sacrificing all of those things in order to be more responsible in the way that you purchase. And the product itself will be compromised. And so I completely challenge that. I really believe that I can make as beautiful, if not more beautiful products, but not in a way that is harmful to the planet.

OUR INTENTIONS WHEN WE BUY

In the coming chapters I talk about the principles we can live by to make beneficial fashion choices. And a lot of sustainability comes down to our intentions when we buy. Remember that this conversation is not just about *what* we buy. The conversation is also around the pieces we currently have. How we can have less and wear it more? How can we appreciate and maintain inspiration with our current wardrobes? This all comes down to styling, learning how to mix and match in ways you might not have thought of. It also comes down to truly enjoying what you wear. Celebrating fabrics, colour and allowing yourself to love what you wear each day.

To be sustainable is now imperative; it is becoming the new normal for the way we need to do things. Just as a culture of fast fashion has grown massively, sustainability is also becoming a new normal. It's our responsibility to be champions for an ethical and considered wardrobe. When we elevate our understanding of sustainability, and promote it with our fantastic style, people will comment and ask, and that will be your way of being able to talk about this new mindset.

A friend once said to me that culture is defined as 'the way we do things around here'. Sustainability can become the new culture. Newer brands especially are starting with sustainability in mind. They are designing with the end in mind, choosing practices that create minimal waste. Fabrics are chosen that have been produced with new and ecological fibres. The makers of their clothing are valued and given a respectable wage with good working conditions.

There are now many wonderful designers creating clothing that is elegant and made for our professional and personal lives. And in fact these new boundaries create an opportunity because they are setting standards for the future. Now that a group of designers have shown that you can make beautiful clothing which is also respectful of the planet, other designers can come on board and use similar sustainable business models. The upside is that the clothes in our wardrobes can ultimately be sustainable and ethical as well as beautiful.

CHAPTER 34

How to be a conscious consumer

'To know exactly what is the story behind this product. This is authenticity today.' — Simone Cipriani

It's an empowering vision to choose wellbeing for ourselves, others and the planet. To know that this can be a driving force in our lives, and is possible. And knowing we can maintain our standard of elegance at the same time is reassuring. We are finding a new way to be in the world. This new vision also means that each time we are about to buy a new piece of clothing we need to act with a conscious awareness. We need to become a conscious consumer.

The first thing we need is knowledge of what we should look for and how to make better buying decisions. In gaining this knowledge we can then choose with a greater awareness. We can make decisions that will, in some small or large way, have a positive impact on the fashion system. And also lead us to loving our clothes more and feeling good about the things we wear.

TIME TO PAUSE

With greater knowledge, knowing what to buy and how, we will choose clothing that fits us better, that feels better, and has a purpose in our wardrobes. We will also be doing whatever we can to buy pieces that have been made with awareness. Being a conscious consumer challenges us to think differently. Being conscious requires us to pause in the moment when we are about to buy something but don't need it. Or to pause when we are about to throw something out but could perhaps find a better use for it instead.

Being able to pause takes energy. It's like standing still in the current of a river. And yet this one action has an impact. It forces the current of the river to flow in a different direction and shift its movement around us. So if we don't buy that item, or choose to be more considered with where our money goes, this will have a flow-on effect. We will be supporting positive change in the industry. If we can review our habits and values around fashion then we have much greater power to decide how we actually want to engage with fashion. Take a look at the values you have when shopping. Ask yourself, what causes me to make the final decision? Am I driven by price? By how it feels?

Being a conscious consumer means asking if we really need to buy something new. It is being prepared to take a greater view on how and what we consume. To ask, do we really need as many clothes as are considered the norm? And what implications do our purchases have?

When we make the decision to purchase with awareness we are choosing to shop with a set of values. We allow those values to guide our actions. So let's take it to the next level and choose a set of values that aligns with a greater view. Let's choose values that support how we want to feel and look as well as our greatest vision for the future of the planet. Because ultimately, if we choose more ethical and sustainably made garments we are supporting a change for the better in the fashion industry.

CHAPTER 35

The devil is in the detail

'When we select fabrics and yarns, we are making choices about better farming practices, greener dyes and more innovative production.' — Eileen Fisher

When we understand the journey that someone has taken to become successful, we appreciate that person even more. It's the same with fashion; as we learn about the stories behind our garments it gives them greater significance and meaning. On the other side, when we learn what happens to some of our clothes in the process of being made it can open our eyes to parts of the industry we will no longer choose to endorse.

Each piece of clothing we own has a trail and a story. When we buy a garment it's not just the product that we invest in, we also invest in the people who made it and the techniques that were used. Sometimes this is an empowering thing and other times it's a trail of environmental and human mistreatment. This is what we need to consider if we are going to use our voices and actions towards a better fashion future.

TAKING STOCK

You and I can facilitate change in the industry simply by looking for information that will empower our fashion choices. This all starts with taking stock of our own fashion footprint. When I look at clothes I bought before learning about fashion and sustainability, I realise now that I put little thought into where they came from. I cared a lot about their aesthetic and whether they were well made, but beyond that there was not a second thought. Because I had always eaten healthy and bought organic produce, when organic cotton came onto the scene and became popular I began to buy organic cotton in t-shirts and other apparel. But this was more so because of my existing lifestyle and preference for organics rather than actively seeking out new information. Now that I am aware, I look for as much information as I can before making a purchase. If a brand demonstrates sustainability and ethical labour clearly in their marketing I am more likely to click further and find out more. I rarely buy new clothes, and if I do it is usually from a smaller designer who is producing locally or whom I know has a substantial commitment to a better world. I also shop for vintage clothing, I find the most beautiful pieces of great quality for a price I am prepared to pay.

Imagine walking into a store or looking online at a brand's current collection and being able to read all about how their clothes are made. Wouldn't that put you in a better position to buy or not buy from them?

If we make the effort to look behind the curtain we will come to a whole new appreciation of our garments. It will inspire so much more respect for the brands who are producing with sound and caring business models. Let's become inquisitive about the details: the composition of the fabrics, the production and so on. Not many fashion brands out there disclose much information but with some digging you will be surprised with what you find. And you will truly appreciate a garment that aligns with your values when you find it.

CHAPTER 36

We can't flip the switch of change overnight

'If you want to change a paradigm, you can't do it alone.'
— Marie-Claire Daveu, Chief Sustainability Officer, Kering

The conversation around the harmful environmental and social impacts of the fashion industry is a big one. There are many levels of change that have to take place, and it's easy to become disheartened by all the work that's needed to truly make headway. However, it's important to understand that every positive action we make *does* count. If we focus on this, we will be more inspired to become part of the movement towards change.

If fashion is one of the most polluting industries in the world then it has to be one to make radical change. As a whole, the industry has taken steps to become more environmentally friendly and we need to acknowledge this. Unfortunately, the amount of work already done does not equal the amount of change necessary to turn the tide on the industry's environmental and humanitarian impact.

The entire fashion industry knows it needs to adopt sustainable practices and become more transparent, and yet not all companies are taking action. The ones who are taking action are doing so in varying degrees, and this is where it starts to become more complex. There are many people, communities, livelihoods and industries involved in the fashion business and its complex supply chains around the world. For each of them to be made more sustainable it's going to take a very high level of commitment.

AT A TIPPING POINT

We really are at a tipping point in terms of climate change and the diminishing of the earth's resources. The fashion industry must gather its energies if it's going to make the impact needed. The analogy of turning a ship is perfect. It takes a huge amount of effort and time to stop a big ship and then turn it around towards a new destination. But when the ship starts to turn it is unstoppable. It's the same for where we are at with fashion. We are at that point where everyone needs to get on board the movement because the ship is turning.

It's not enough for a few brands to shift to a better fabric or give customers the option to bring their used clothes back for recycling. There needs to be systemic and radical change. If the fashion industry is not moving at a quick enough pace then we need to emplore them to act. It's the brands that will have to change, and we can be the ones to force them to do so. Realising that the change cannot happen overnight, it's even more important that we get started now.

CHAPTER 37

Getting our human on

'The minute we all join hands and have the same mission and the same honest approach, we'll get there.'
— Stella McCartney

Our personal fashion footprint is made up of the garments we own and those that we buy. It is connected to so many lives and natural resources. It can be easy when something is out of sight to go about our daily lives without a second thought. But just because we don't feel or see the work that has gone into our garments doesn't mean there weren't many hands and hours of effort that went into producing them.

BRINGING PEACE OF MIND

Just imagine hearing that the women and men who were once working in chemical factories that treated our clothes were now able to work in a garment industry that used natural dyes. Wouldn't that bring peace of mind? If we heard that denim production, which is one of the most toxic industries, had now reformed and converted to environmentally friendly production. That would also cause a big sign of relief.

Picture the young children across the world who come from families caught in poverty who could now be taken care of properly while their parents work. That these young children of five years or younger, who once had to lie on a factory floor while their parents work, could now play with their friends during the day because their parents were being given fair working conditions and proper wages.

When we hear a story of blue skies returning in a city that was once polluted or animals repopulating areas where they were going extinct, it immediately brings up good feelings, doesn't it? Considering the wellbeing of the planet is a great incentive to rethink our fashion. If you care for the environment, which I'm sure you do, then call on your best experiences in pristine places and allow that to be your guide for how you want to see the world. Allow that to lead your fashion choices.

Let's decide to get our human on and remember that without a healthy planet our daily lives will look very different. We are reliant on nature; it supports us and enables us to eat, drink and be healthy. It's up to us to make decisions that support this cycle.

Every time we choose to repair a garment rather than send it to charity we are making a choice that's beneficial for nature. Every time we chose to pay that little bit more for a piece of clothing and ensure someone is being paid fairly we are getting our human on. Putting ourselves in the shoes of the people who make our clothes, we can ask, *is this something I would want for myself, and if not, what can I do to support them?*

With this book, take the tools you learn to curate your own fashion for the better. Aim to be more conscious with your fashion choices and choose to use them for good. Let's decide to make fundamental changes to our fashion footprint and make decisions from the heart. Having nice clothes and things is fantastic, but when our decisions have the ability to shift the way fashion impacts people it puts a whole new spin on things. Kindness and compassion must lead the way if we are to help those people in developing countries whose job it is to make our clothes.

PART VI

It's time to take action

'You know the greatest thing is passion, without it what have you got?'

—Diana Vreeland

THIS IS THE PART where we truly get to make a difference. Now we get to take action. We are at the point where real change happens, within our own wardrobes, our hearts and our wallets. Where we really start rethinking our relationship with fashion.

Are you curious? Have you already peeked into the upcoming chapters to see what's in store? Over the coming chapters we will take a look at all the ways we can make empowered and conscious personal choices. How our personal style can be the greatest reflection of how we personally want to look and feel and how it can also be a vote for the wellbeing of humanity and the environment.

We are going to look at our beliefs and values around fashion and whether they fit in with our newfound knowledge. We will also ask whether our personal style is truly congruent with who we are and how we live our lives. We will talk about the types of clothing we own, and get into the nitty gritty like the fit of a garment, the fabrics and what they are made of. Taking our budget into account we talk about how to invest in our clothes in the right way and how to take care of them. Each of these are so important if we truly want to be making beneficial choices.

There is so much information to cover when it comes to choosing the right garments and understanding the environmental and humanitarian impacts of the ones we currently own. This starts with the fibres contained in the fabric our clothes are made of, such as cotton or wool, how they are sourced, and where they come from.

In this *doing* section of the book I touch very lightly on these areas; if you are looking for detailed information, please make sure to head over to the resources section of my website.

There truly is so much to cover, lots of doing and lots of practical information. In the following chapters there are a lot of questions we have to ask. This is because so much of what we need to do when we rethink our fashion involves asking better questions. But don't let this daunt you. It's an enlivening process and so beneficial in the long run. When we have more knowledge and it aligns with our actions we truly have a powerful force for change.

CHAPTER 38

Start by rethinking your relationship with fashion

'You can be gorgeous at thirty, charming at forty, and irresistible for the rest of your life.' — Coco Chanel

There are moments in our lives when a new perspective takes hold of us and it impacts the way we go forward. I hope what you have read so far has started to create some movement within you. That it has stirred a desire to make conscious choices for the wellbeing of humanity and our planet as a result.

To rethink our relationship with fashion means we need to elevate our awareness. It's time to put the desire for wellbeing at the forefront of every decision. I know this is a lofty goal, and at the same time it can also be very practical. When we remind ourselves of who we want to be and how we want to act it can guide our decisions and actions. I mentioned earlier that dynamic change like this is incremental, but what greater way is there to make decisions?

WHAT'S YOUR RELATIONSHIP WITH FASHION?

The first step towards rethinking our fashion is to look at our values. Before any social or environmental incentive, we need to ask ourselves what our own relationship with fashion is.

Our complicated love affair with fashion has been carved out over many years. Our entire lifetime actually. It's made up of social and cultural influences. How we dress has been influenced by how we grew up, our friends, peers and relationships. The career expectations. The activities we are involved in and hobbies we pursue. And then there are the influences I'm sure you're already well aware of: media, magazines, celebrities, and now influencers all trying to promote the 'ideal look'.

These marketed, curated images aim to carve out an aspirational ideal. But shouldn't this manufactured ideal make us want to look further for our own authentic beauty? That is what it has done for me. But it definitely took some time. It takes time to unhook ourselves from the social norms of weight, height and size.

Fortunately, this is all being tipped on its head as voices of diversity and inclusivity are loudly heard these days. However, for us to truly remove ourselves from these ideals we need to honour ourselves. If we feel beautiful then we are beautiful, handsome, attractive and sexy.

On the other side, the clothes we wear do also impact how we feel. Whether we realise it or not. The wrong shapes of clothing, the wrong fit and wrong colours can make us look and feel unbalanced. When we look in the mirror we may not know why we feel uncomfortable, but if we took off that outfit and put one on that was the perfect fit, size, shape and colour, it would instantly transform how we feel.

SELF-IMAGE

Where do all our fashion choices begin? They begin with our self-image. Each of us has a multi-faceted relationship in this department. On those days where lipstick and eyeliner or a fresh coat of mascara aren't going to cut it, what is it that makes us feel our best? It's our sense of self that enables us to step out the door even in those moments when we are feeling down about certain areas of our life, or are dealing with setbacks.

The degree to which we value ourselves also influences the way we take care of our bodies, our lifestyle choices, personal time, the types of clothes we choose, how we look after our clothes, and how we take care of our appearance.

It is really valuable to take some time to contemplate the ways in which our self-image influences these decisions. If we are uncomfortable within, this feeling can dictate just how much we are willing to take care of our appearance — or not. It can influence our shopping habits. Sometimes it can make us buy too much, or it can make us put ourselves at the end of the priority list. When we are out of balance, our lives go out of balance.

In my experience, the more I have come to value myself the better decisions I make. This means buying clothing that I adore. It's choosing the better pieces that make me look and feel fantastic. It's choosing clothing that represents how I truly want to feel, clothing that makes me feel beautiful, confident and feminine. It's buying any new items in a considered way, and at the same time allowing myself to have nice things.

BODY IMAGE, SIZE AND STYLE

What else has a big impact on our relationship with fashion? It's our association with body image, with size and style. For the longest time we have been dictated to about the size we 'should' be in order to be beautiful and feel beautiful. While we have always known that this is a load of rubbish, we are still influenced by it.

We are influenced when we can't find clothing in our size, and it can affect how we shop and what we choose. Sometimes it leads to less-than-ideal purchases. Well, this is the age of truth. And the truth is we are all beautiful. We all have fantastic features. We just need to know how to accentuate them. We also need to know how to find the right pieces. Once we know the basics of how to dress for our body shape then personal style becomes so much easier.

Knowing the basics of body shape and proportion is essential. When we know how to create balance for our size and height, it's so much easier to create a winning look. This in turn gives us confidence because we end up choosing more of the garments that bring out our best.

GETTING YOUR STYLE RIGHT

These are all essential elements that can transform our relationship with fashion. It's just like with tennis: when you get the technique right, hitting a great forehand or backhand comes as a consequence. It's the same with personal style. Once you truly know the shapes and styles that suit you, you will find a whole new flair. It will also futureproof your fashion purchases; you will want to take care of your garments so they last longer so you can wear them more. This process will refine your appreciation of fashion.

Why do I focus on understanding these principles? Because they help you understand and appreciate how attractive and beautiful you really are. When we feel confident we make better decisions, and this ultimately can create a more satisfying wardrobe of clothes. Once we have this, we go a long way towards reducing waste and minimising harmful decisions. Decisions that waste our personal resources and those of the planet. It all starts with us.

Focus on your own personal style. This includes your lifestyle, your needs and your personality. Know how you really want to look and feel in the clothing you wear. Once you understand this you can carve out a collection of clothing that will serve you in the long run. A collection that will be 100% congruent with who you are and one you will be able to build and adapt over time. Each piece will complement your overall look and you will have invested wisely.

In this way, your relationship with fashion will very much reflect the best version of you. It will also be a considered approach and will ensure you build your own sustainable fashion collection.

Getting the basics into order is so important. It's essential for a more authentic representation of who you are and how you want to express yourself in the world. This in turn will impact your entire life. A greater appreciation of your own self, along with a fabulous understanding of the clothes that suit you, will go a long way to you making beneficial decisions and enjoying every outfit you choose to wear.

CHAPTER 39

Make a commitment

'Remain true to yourself and your philosophy.'
— Giorgio Armani

Before we go any further we need to consolidate our thoughts and feelings. If we are going to truly rethink our fashion and then take action, there needs to be a firm resolution. If we want to make a change, we need to make a commitment to ourselves.

As I mentioned in the first part of the book, it's not going to be easy but it's going to be worth it. It requires that we put in the effort needed, that we make the changes and acquire the knowledge needed. It will be worth it because you will be making choices that benefit you personally as well as the environment and the people who make your clothes. You will be making conscious choices that will provide a positive contribution overall.

Putting all these things together can sound like a big ask. And I hope you're not getting overwhelmed. It all starts with making a commitment. And from there any fashion action we take will be in line with that commitment.

BREAK EXISTING HABITS

Sometimes we need to break existing habits, and I have a personal example to illustrate. A while ago I was shopping online for a vintage item and saw a beautiful dress that would work perfectly with what I currently own. However, when I looked more closely at the details of the garment, underneath the size and dimensions was the composition of the fabric. To me, the image of the dress looked like it was made of wool, however when I read the notes, it was actually polyester. Aside from not liking the way polyester feels on my skin, it is also a type of plastic as I mentioned earlier, and I have made a decision not to purchase it as much as possible. This is why in the end I decided not to buy it.

There were a few ways to look at the environmental impact if I was to buy this dress. Firstly, it was vintage which meant it was going to be reused instead of going to landfill. So that was great. Then there is the fabrication, or what it was made of. Personally I choose natural fibres because they feel better on my skin, which means I wear them more often and keep them for longer.

Also, polyester is not biodegradable and has an impact on the environment if it ends up in landfill. (There is an argument that polyester can actually be recycled much more easily than natural fibres like wool, however let's not worry about the nitty gritty too much here.) Taking all this into consideration, you can see that every decision has an impact and it's up to us to take a stand. Even one small step, one small choice towards sustainability is a positive one.

It's also a positive step for the enjoyment and longevity of our wardrobes. The commitments we decide on ultimately need to make it easier for us to take care of and appreciate the clothes we do have as well as guide any future purchases. I have made my own commitments and am refining them all the time. Some of the commitments I have made are:

- Buy from brands and designers who care about people and the process.

- Invest in good-quality pieces that will last many years.

- Make sure a garment has a purpose before I buy.

- Minimise the purchase of polyester and manmade fibres.

- Make sure my clothing is made of sustainably sourced fibres and fabrics.

- Buy locally made and sourced garments.

- Buy more vintage.

- Repair as soon as I see an issue.

- Buy only sustainably and ethically sourced animal fibres like wool and cashmere.

- Take garments that I no longer wear to the tailor so they will fit correctly, be the right length, shape and so on.

What commitments will you make? Maybe you will pledge that you will no longer buy stuff you won't wear. Or you may decide that from now on, when you wear something you must love it and truly look fantastic. Perhaps you will commit to stop buying from fast fashion brands, or you may choose to invest more in quality rather than quantity.

Deciding to approach fashion can start with one decision. I was recently watching an interview led by The Business of Fashion where Gabriela Hearst, one of the leading designers in the sustainability field, spoke about how we can approach it. I'm paraphrasing here, but she said it takes practice: you start with something achievable and then as you achieve it you go to the next stage and the next stage, and it's a never-ending journey. So all it takes is that one commitment to get on board with the movement.

These commitments are personal. Take some time to think about what you have read so far and what it means to you. Put aside a small amount of time; it could be five minutes or half an hour. Use these quiet moments to write down your intentions before we go any further, and in this way you can make your commitment in whatever way works for you.

CHAPTER 40

The reality of how little we need versus how much we buy

'Buy less. Choose well. Make it last.' — Vivienne Westwood

There is a statistic that, on average, we only wear 20% of the clothes we own. Some say that this amount is even less, but either way it means the rest of our clothes are for red carpets, galas and extreme sports or that we simply need to adjust our shopping habits.

What are the reasons we buy too many clothes or the wrong clothes? For some people it's buying on a whim, maybe with a friend, getting caught up in the excitement of the moment. For others it can be a lack of knowledge and not really understanding what suits them which leads to the wrong purchases. And for some women it's simply the joy of shopping that can get a little out of hand.

The reality is that many of us wear a small set of garments over and again in different ways. It's the easy garments that we know fit and that we can rely on to make us look good. Perhaps we stumbled across these garments by chance, buying them because we simply liked them but afterwards realising what a winner they actually were.

It's those winning garments that we want to repeat, to buy similar styles in different fabrics and colours if we need. But overall, we really do require less clothing. It also comes down to lifestyle; many times we have a routine in our life that calls for certain types of clothing. Even though we may think we need more variety, often we are proving to ourselves that we need less than we own simply by our current habit of wearing only 20% of our wardrobe.

BEING MORE MINDFUL

There is also a trend starting to take place where people are buying less. People are wanting to be more mindful of what and how they buy. This is particularly visible with millennials, who would prefer to spend their money on experiences or invest in a social cause they believe in. Overall, millennials are very socially conscious and are seeing the impact fashion is having on the planet, and they want to do something about it. They are opting to buy less and are creating other innovative ways to access clothes that don't involve ownership, whereby they can still have variety but don't need to own as much.

I came to understand just how little I needed when I was living in a small remote village in India over 20 years ago. During those four years I worked in a very focused environment; I also practised meditation and studied the ancient yogic texts. The focus of my daily routine was turned from the external to the internal. From the material to a life of reflection, contemplation, and an appreciation of simplicity.

In the beginning it took some time to adjust, as you can imagine. There was no TV, no computer, no wifi and no cell phones at the time. It took a while for me to be comfortable with this lack of external stimulation, but as my stay extended I found that my mind was calm and I was able to be more present. Life was very simple and at the same time so fulfilling.

Living in a different culture, it was also respectful to wear the local dress, and so in the first few days I had to borrow pieces from newfound friends before getting the opportunity to buy my own. I remember walking down the road in the monsoon rain to a local store which sold saris and salwar kameez, a type of tunic and pants. I was not used to the unstructured style of these clothes, which left no definition of the body and had so much fabric.

The first pieces I bought were functional but didn't feel so beautiful. The fabrics were scratchy or made of polyester which made me hot, and the prints — well, let's just say they were not what I would normally buy. Eventually I bought some pieces in Mumbai that I loved; they were made of a really soft cotton, and had block colours with beautiful detailing from different regions of India. I remember a gorgeous cotton bottle-green piece from Rajasthan. It was fitted in the bodice with soft, slim sleeves that tapered at the wrist. From the waist it gently billowed out with an elegant fullness. I remember wearing that outfit so often.

As life settled, I had a small collection of clothing that I just loved so much, with exotic fabrics, colours and some with delicate embroidery. The daily routine was simple. I found as my senses were less focused on the external I became more still inside, and with this stillness came greater feelings of ease. The need to be entertained by my environment decreased, and I was happy whether talking with friends or sitting quietly alone. This kind of lifestyle is not a usual one for a woman in her 20s — and yes, I have lived an unconventional life — but the experience was so valuable, in fact life changing. The satisfaction I get now from simply being in nature or getting lost in a creative endeavour like designing are to me what makes life meaningful.

Coming back to the West was a challenge, with the focus on the material, success and performance. It took time to adjust and integrate, but I managed to do it. And funnily enough, my time in India created this deep love of fabrics, and fashion. While I was in India it got to the point where I realised I really wanted to be in fashion.

Being in a culture that was so rich with artisan traditions was truly inspiring. I got so much joy and inspiration from the celebration of colour, exquisite fabrics and incredible details that were created by hand from people who had developed skills over a lifetime. This experience had ignited my love of textiles and fashion, and is what brought me to the industry.

Fast forward to today and fashion is very different. Since the invention of fast fashion, the value of a garment has been left behind. Cheap prices and trendy items have become the norm, and this new system has created a disposable culture. Fast fashion supports the belief that you can buy something, wear it once and throw it out without consequences.

There is no connection to the maker or the design process, and there really is no story behind the garment.

The problem with buying clothing in this way lies in the attitude. The issue is whether or not we value what we have. I remember talking with a friend whose family is very wealthy, and she was telling me that her mother has many garments still with the price tag on. These items have never been worn, and may stay that way. There are so many stories like this. Another story I heard recently was of a woman who used to buy a new pair of shoes every week, and they were not your entry-level variety either.

I understand wanting to buy something new, and the feeling of reinvention and freshness that a new design in a new colour can give. At the same time, there has to be a point at which it ceases to be satisfying. A point where we no longer need any more. And my question is, are we really satisfied? What is this need to keep consuming?

THE FUTURE OF FASHION

There is also a group of fashion brands who are asking people to buy less clothing. You would think that it is counterintuitive, right? To be producing clothes in order to tell people not to buy them? When you dig a little deeper the purpose and intention becomes clear.

There is a men's clothing brand in the United States called ASKET, and on their website there is a section dedicated to their methodology. It comes under the navigation tab titled 'Our Pursuit', which I love because it defines that they really are on a mission for change. At the top of the page this is what they say:

The world doesn't need another fashion brand.

And certainly doesn't need more clothing.

Garments, products of delicate labour and precious resources, have lost their value.

We buy more and use them less than ever — packing our wardrobes, filling landfills and fuelling incinerators.

All at the expense of our society and planet.

ASKET exists to end this.

We don't design for seasons, we create for forever.

When something isn't perfect we improve it.

When something is broken we mend it.

Our definition of progress is reduced wardrobes.

Built on pieces that will stand the test of time.

Both in craftsmanship and design.

We envision a world free of fast consumption.

A world with less clutter, less waste, less smoke and mirrors.

ASKET. The pursuit of less.

What a wonderful statement, and I can tell you that there are more and more brands coming on board with a similar message. They understand that we all need clothes, and they want to offer an alternative where we can buy clothing that is made with really well-thought-out design and fabrics so that we will love wearing them. So that we will have multiple ways to wear them for multiple purposes. These brands are also built on sustainable and ethical practices. It really is the future of fashion.

Now I'm not suggesting that you only have a minimal wardrobe of 30 items which the capsule wardrobe movement recommends. My view is that this can feel a bit constricting, and to be honest doesn't leave much room for personality, colour, fabrics and flair. At the same time, I believe our clothes must have a purpose, and most of all we must be wearing them. We just need to be smarter about the clothes we buy.

If I asked you to pull out the clothes you wear the most, how many garments would you show me? Does it represent the small proportion I mentioned earlier? And of those clothes, which ones do you feel most confident in? This could be an even smaller number. I'm guessing the clothes you wear regularly are the ones most relevant for your lifestyle. These are probably the items which meet your needs, including the roles you need to play in your life. And they also make you feel like the woman or man you feel you are or want to be.

Why not focus on having only the clothes that truly represent your style and personality? The ones that fit you like a glove and highlight all your best features. These are the garments you need. Why not test out a new approach? I challenge you to come to an agreement with yourself that once you reach a point where you have the clothes you truly need and love that you will not buy for as long as possible. And when you *do* buy some new clothing, to make sure that they will align with your values.

CHAPTER 41

Better habits will lead to better decisions

'The more you know, the less you need.'
— Yvon Chouinard, Patagonia

For many of us when it comes to buying clothes we can often be on auto-pilot. We all have habits that we've developed over time, but in alignment with the entire message of this book perhaps it's time to rethink those habits. The main reason for this is that with extra information we can make better decisions. And these new actions will require new habits.

Each of us has our own individual habits with fashion. We have routines and rituals for when we buy clothing and how we like to buy. Even if those routines are that we only replace something when it wears out, that itself is a routine. This habit in itself can lead to impulse buying because all of a sudden we need something *now*, and when we go out and look for it there's nothing we love but we end up buying because we need it.

Some of us are a different kind of impulse buyer, buying frequently but preferring not to plan and instead to buy when we see something we like. Others are bulk buyers, going out for a big shop once or twice a year and that's it. Others buy minimally, only a couple of items here and there, depending when there is a need. Some of us only shop in the sales, and some of us see a picture of someone wearing an item that we love and our mind is made up — we go and buy it. For others, it could be a combination of a few of these.

No matter what your normal habits are, now is the time to take a closer look to decide if they are really working for you, and how you might be able to adjust them so they meet more of your fashion goals and needs.

WHAT'S WORKING FOR YOU?

If we want to make better decisions we first need to understand how we make them. Only then can we choose to do more of what works and less of what derails us. Some of the questions we can ask ourselves are:

- When do I usually go shopping for clothes?

- What are the things that derail me?

- Under what circumstances do I shop? Is it a need? An addiction? When I'm bored or stressed?

- Where do I shop? And are those brands actually appropriate for me?

- Do I know what I need or want when I go shopping?

- Do I know what suits me?

- What are the brands that have the clothes that fit me?

- Are there things that stop me from shopping? For example, I never find what I'm looking for, or I don't know where to start?

From these questions you should be able to get a good idea of what doesn't serve you well and what is already working to your advantage. After gathering this information, you may want to go a little further by asking:

- How many clothes do I actually need?

- Can I shop with more of a strategy?

- What does that strategy look like?

- What can I do so that I'm buying more sustainably?

- What brands can I buy from that are sustainable and ethical and also suit my style?

- What are the ways I can be more sustainable with the clothes I currently own?

The main point is to understand the times when you go shopping and it doesn't work out for you, and why. Perhaps this means you need a more detailed strategy. Not a rigid strategy, but just more of an understanding of your needs and whether you are really buying in alignment with them.

CREATING BETTER HABITS

Better habits mean being able to understand when we are buying something that we won't wear or keep for long. It means understanding which fabrics work best for us and sticking to those. It means choosing to be more considered overall. Over time, as you build a wardrobe that's more satisfying, one that is built for longevity, the less you will need to think about clothes or fashion. It's all about building a collection of clothes you truly love. Your wardrobe can become a playground.

One woman said to me recently that she has stopped buying clothing because it seems too hard to research the brands that will suit her style as well as being ethical and sustainable. This is where it takes greater effort in the beginning. It will take some time to learn what really is good for you and the environment and what isn't. But imagine as you start to find the right brands – you will actually find that your approach gets simpler, and becomes more successful and satisfying.

Having tighter boundaries actually makes the results more exciting, because when you know what you are after and you do find those pieces it will be so worth it. Shopping for clothes will become easier. For example, you can start to build a little database of brands you love. Over time, you will have them to reference and choose from. As you become better able to spot a fashion brand that's truly offering a sustainable alternative over one that merely spouts marketing messages, it will become like second nature to find what you are looking for.

Better habits also include the ways we take care of our current clothing. For example, when we have a neat, clean and organised wardrobe, our clothing lasts longer, because it is being taken care of. When we wash garments in the right way they also last longer. Rotating your clothing rather than wearing something over and over also extends its life.

Looking at your wardrobe in this way, you may also ask if you feel satisfied with your current wardrobe. You can start to think about building one that truly meets your needs. One which is also ethical and has the least impact on the environment. These are all the things that come up as we try to reorient ourselves to a new way of thinking about fashion.

We can't create new habits if we don't know what our values and goals are. Know how you like to shop and tailor your habits so you can still get what you need but in a more sustainable way. Follow these guidelines for more beneficial decisions:

- Know the sustainable, ethical brands you would like to buy from.

- Have a clear understanding of the types of clothing that work well for you.

- Have a clear understanding of the types of clothing you want to invest in.

- Be considered.

- Buy sparingly.

- When in doubt, don't buy.

- Take care of the clothing you currently own.

This approach will give you greater satisfaction. It will also help you protect your clothing investment as well as plan for any new items. Overall, better habits definitely do lead to better decisions.

CHAPTER 42

Drive change by asking better questions

'If people asked for it, it can happen tomorrow.'
— Bruno Pieters

You'll notice throughout this book we have to ask a lot of questions. The reason we do this is so that we don't take things at face value. For example, if I was to put five similar pairs of blue jeans in front of you, they would not all be created equally. But how are we to know if we don't ask the right questions? And how will we be able to drive change if we don't have the right information?

Those five similar pairs of blue jeans may end up looking very different depending on how they were made and who made them. If we want to choose the more ethical and sustainable option we need to find out more information. Japan makes some of the most beautiful denim in the world, however imagine buying a pair of jeans and then finding out that the company had been contributing to the pollution of one of Japan's most famous rivers for over 50 years. Would that change your opinion and experience of those jeans? Would it change how you bought jeans in the future?

Or what about human rights? What would you do if one of the companies that produced a pair of those blue jeans was having them made in a factory where workers were expected to stay late into the night to meet unrealistic targets and were also denied lunch breaks because of these deadlines? That also would change our opinion of those jeans.

The thing is that most of the time we are not provided with this kind of information. And with all the knowledge we now have about what ethical and sustainable clothing truly is, don't we want to make sure that our clothing purchases contribute to a better world?

We can do this by asking questions before we make a purchase. When we see a garment and know nothing about the dyes that were used or the people who made it, we can turn to the brand that is selling it and ask for more information. Just by asking questions, it's possible a brand will stand up and take notice. It may not happen straight away, but odds are if you are asking questions then other people will be also. When a fashion brand starts receiving enough questions it's possible they will feel the need to do something about it.

ANJU

Anju is a garment worker in Bangladesh; she is only paid 37 cents an hour to make our clothes. Her wages are less than the minimum wage in Bangladesh, and deductions are made if she falls behind on the steep targets given to her. Anju's job is to stitch the front and back of sweaters together, and she is paid on the number of sweaters she stitches not the quality of work that she does. Anju's daughters live with her parents, and she only gets to see them twice a year because she cannot afford to keep them with her. Anju says that if she had a proper wage she could have her daughters live with her (Oxfam).

This is one of many stories of women, and also men, who are trapped in the cycle of poverty. Even if big companies were to pass the entire cost of living wages of all workers on to consumers, Deloitte estimates this would increase the price of a piece of clothing sold in Australia by just 1%. That is just 10 cents extra for a $10 t-shirt. And a $10 price tag does not account for the environmental implications, nor denote a quality garment.

If we were to ask questions and also communicate that it means more to us that workers are paid fairly than to get a cheap t-shirt, and even that we are happy to incur that extra expense in order for it to happen, a brand might feel compelled to take action. It all comes down to asking questions.

BECOMING ENGAGED

It may feel at times like we don't have much power to persuade fashion brands and companies to shift their way of working. The truth is that we can use our voices to promote change. We can question the current practices of brands we normally engage with and slowly they will be forced to stand up and take action.

I'm sure you have your favourite brands. Do you know much about them? Perhaps you can become inquisitive and show your interest in their company values. Become engaged. If you have a relationship with a particular staff member at a local boutique, why not start a conversation and find out more about how they produce their clothes? The best way is to start locally with genuine concern and compassion.

Many brands are only going to share the information we seek once the demand is high enough. We can begin a narrative with brands by asking three questions. These three questions have become the backbone of the Fashion Revolution agenda. Fashion Revolution is a global movement and their vision is: 'A global fashion industry that conserves and restores the environment and values people over growth and profit.'

The answers to these questions can reveal just how ethical and environmentally conscious a business is. And if a brand is not able to tell you, these are the best starting points to begin a conversation. These questions are an important cornerstone for change:

- What's in my clothes?

- Who made my clothes?

- Where did my clothes come from?

Let's look at these.

What's in my clothes?

By asking this simple question, you open up a door of possible answers which can lead to other questions. For example, if you were to ask 'what fabric is my clothing made of?', you may find out that it is made of viscose, which has been considered as a more sustainable option. Viscose is also known as rayon, and is made of wood pulp. However, depending on the type of viscose and where it came from, it has varying impact. Did you know that the fashion industry is responsible for cutting down about 150 million trees per year (Canopy)? Unfortunately, these trees often come from endangered and ancient forests. There is now an initiative by an NGO called Canopy to eliminate fibres coming from these forests and to instead find new alternatives to produce the same fabric.

This is why we need to ask questions, to dig deeper and become more informed. So, to complete the example, first you ask, 'what fabric is this?' And then you can ask where the fabric came from, and how the fibres that made the fabric were sourced.

Our clothing, depending how it is made, can also come with a host of chemicals and treatment processes that were used along the way. Unless we ask better questions, how are we to know?

Who made my clothes?

This simple question can also open up many different answers. Is the brand telling you about their commitment to ethical labour? Are they telling you about their workers? Some brands will show you pictures of their factories on their website, or tell you about their fair pay and fair work promises. Many fashion brands have no idea about their supply chain, including the conditions of the factories that make the clothes. This is why we also need to ask and probe deeper.

Some fashion brands tout ethical practices and can show you pictures on their website of people finishing off their garments in local factories, but this doesn't mean the whole line of production was done under the one roof. It could mean the initial construction of their garments was done in factories where they have no knowledge of the conditions, in places that are not audited by reputable industry bodies.

Behind our clothes there is a long chain of people and stories; we need fashion companies to tell us more of these. There are the farmers, spinners, weavers, the people who sew our clothes; there are millions of factory workers around the world. Being truly transparent means being able to tell you all of this information. When we know about the people at every stage of production and creation, our clothing takes on meaning. It also brings greater transparency and accountability to the clothing we buy.

Where did my clothes come from?

This question helps us to find out more detail about the entirety of a business's supply chain. It is about, for example, finding out where the farms were that grew the cotton, or raised the animals that produced the wool for our knitwear. It means being able to tell us about the farming practices and whether they are regenerative or depleting of the environment. Whether the sheep were taken care of ethically or not.

It means finding out about the tanneries that produced the leather if we choose to buy leather goods. Or learning how many times the fabrics and zippers, thread and other elements used to put the fashion item together were flown around the world before they became a product.

WHERE DO YOU FIND THIS INFORMATION?

The first thing you can do to find out this information is to visit the website of the brands you currently buy from. Hopefully they will have a dedicated section on transparency or sustainability. Unfortunately, many businesses don't, which means you will need to dig a little deeper. And if you can't find the information you are looking for then this tells you a lot in itself. Next time you go into the store you can then ask them what their practices are.

If a local business cannot give you the information you are after, there is another option. To get involved vocally. To write a letter or email to the company and ask for a response. Depending on how public you want to be, you can also post on their Facebook page and ask the same questions: 'what's in my clothes?', 'Who makes my clothes?' and 'Where do my clothes come from?' You can publicly ask that the brand commits to setting new sustainable and ethical targets.

This approach may be the longer one, however new solutions will only take place through systemic change. We can definitely choose to take our dollars elsewhere, and I encourage this. True change takes place at the top level and we are the ones to drive this by asking questions and spending carefully.

Acting locally is one of the best ways to create a new economy and drive environmental and humanitarian change. We can choose brands that give us information on their supply chains. These are brands that have a minimal carbon footprint, with fabrics that are sourced locally. This means items have less of a distance to travel to reach our wardrobes. If our clothes are made and sourced locally we will also strengthen our local communities; it will have positive cultural benefits as well as regenerative environmental benefits.

I recently listened to a conversation with designer Gabriella Hearst, who was being interviewed about sustainability and ethical practices. Gabriella Hearst is one of the fierce advocates in this space who from the inception of her brand has understood that sustainability should be in every part of a businesses. When asked if people care and are asking questions, Gabriella Hearst said that recently there have been more and more people writing in, emailing and asking these very questions I have spoken about. They want to know all the details, right down to where the sheep graze and how they are looked after. This shows that the awareness and call for transparency is truly growing.

CHAPTER 43

Be the change you want to see

'Be the change that you wish to see in the world.'
— Mahatma Gandhi

This famous Mahatma Gandhi quote aptly describes the approach that's needed when it comes to rethinking fashion. To truly take this on board you need to decide how you are going to be and act now that you have this new knowledge.

Earlier on we spoke about making a commitment to making new decisions in the future, and now this is about the actions we take. It's one thing to make a commitment, but we show our commitment though action.

If you want to experience something you must become it. For example, if you want the world to be kinder be kind. If you want the planet to be healthier, start making more environmentally friendly decisions. You've got to decide what it is that you want the world to look like and become that.

I was faced with this recently when I was looking to buy a new puffer jacket. I was going to go back to the brand I had bought my last one from until I realised that the down used in that jacket was most likely not ethically sourced. Because I had made the decision I wasn't going to buy clothing that would have involved animal cruelty, after researching the brand I decided I wasn't going to buy from them.

This is an example of how, when we make a decision, our actions and choices that follow need be aligned if we are truly going to make a difference. It takes time for us to gather the knowledge we need to make informed decisions.

The main thing is that we start acting in line with our commitments. That we make choices in alignment with our newfound or existing beliefs. Sustainability is a way of life. It involves the way we approach each moment. It's a time to stand for something. You have to know the changes you want and act on them.

If you're not clear on that then you have no guidelines. So, remember to revisit your commitments so they will inspire your actions day after day.

CHAPTER 44

Take stock of your current wardrobe

'Why do we need every week a new part of clothing? Fashion is a great thing to achieve happiness, to be able to show yourself what you love and all that, but there has to be a way to create something that lasts longer. Something which has got far more beauty, artisanal beauty, and at the same time it's something that stays in the wardrobe for a really long time.'
— Rahul Mishra

Well, now it's time to get started, and the best place to begin is in your wardrobe with the clothes you already own. This is a really insightful exercise. I want it to be fun for you. The main intention is to really understand your values around fashion, to look at what you buy and why. To learn what works for you and what doesn't.

Reviewing our clothes and learning why we wear some clothes and not others is the key to finding out what you truly need and will want to keep forever. I don't mean only owning a minimal amount of items till the end of time. Not at all. Fashion is about creativity and inspiration, and how much and what we own is individual. When I talk about finding what you need, I mean understanding the clothing that works best for your body shape, lifestyle, personal style, as well as what truly suits you.

Let's inspect every element to find out how you can make your current wardrobe more sustainable and enjoyable. I want you to discover:

- the clothes that make you feel your best and why

- the clothing that fits you the best

- the fabrics that have the most longevity (including comfort and durability)

- the clothes you don't wear and why

- the mistakes you have made, and will stop

- how to relove and restyle clothing you had forgotten

- a positive use for unloved clothing

- the clothing you need – pieces you can add that will be sustainable, quality additions you will want to keep for many years.

I invite you to find some available time in your calendar where you can block out a decent part of the day, perhaps even a whole day depending on how big your wardrobe or wardrobes are. You want time to be able to review and rethink what you currently own.

GET SORTED

Oh, a wardrobe audit, you may be thinking. Well, yes and no. The intention of this process is more about self-awareness. It's an honest exploration to understand your fashion habits so you can adjust anything that might not be working well for you. You will also learn what truly does work and find ways to improve on that. Along the way you will end up putting your clothing into categories and sorting them out so that you can establish a new base of a truly long-lasting and satisfying wardrobe. It's time to rethink your relationship with your fashion in a practical, hands-on way.

So let's get started.

Identify the clothes you love and wear the most

Firstly, I want you to start by taking the clothes out of your wardrobe that you love and wear regularly. Not the ones that you wear but don't feel comfortable in. Only the clothes where you truly feel confident, attractive, amazing, at ease and able to get stuff done when you're wearing them. Depending on the size of your wardrobe, this may take some time. You can look at them outfit by outfit or take them out all at once.

How you do this also depends on how many clothes you actually wear, but if we consider the statistic that we wear an average of 20% of the clothes we own, it may not take as long as you expect. So take them out and lay them on your bed or a sofa or hang them on a rack if you have that option.

Now take out a notepad and write down the key elements that you love about each garment, or each outfit. You can break them up into categories if you want, like work, casual, formal. You may find a lot of positives and things that you want to continue doing. You may also find a few gaps, or pieces of clothing that you need to complete this winning collection, so write that down too.

I want you to also look for the quality of these pieces. Is there something in particular that sets them apart from the others? Perhaps it's the design, or the fabrics, or the way they sit on your body perfectly. I want you to note down who the designers are that you buy from the most and why. Write down especially the most sustainable elements, like any organic cotton garments, artisan pieces bought directly from the maker, clothes made of natural dyes, wool that was sourced sustainably.

I know I can comfortably make do with a few key outfits over the week by interchanging pieces and wearing different shoes and accessories. This may be different for you, but my main need is clothing that makes me feel feminine, beautiful and the slimmest version of myself. The clothes I gravitate towards are well cut and made of fabrics which feel soft, luxurious and drape in all the right places.

Identify the unworn and unloved items

Next, take out the clothes you have barely or never worn and lay them all out to be reviewed. On your notepad, write down all the reasons why each piece goes unloved and unworn. Here are some reasons:

- It could be that you don't like the fabric and it doesn't feel right.

- It never actually fit you properly to begin with.

- It was a 'what was I thinking?' purchase. (And if so, why?)

- It came apart or got holes quickly.

- You don't actually know why but you just don't like to wear it.

There is a lot of information contained in these purchases; they highlight the mistakes so you don't make them again. You need to understand why you bought them and why you don't wear them. This is the area you really want to understand if you are going to build a truly sustainable wardrobe. We want to aim for a collection of clothing where you wear 80%, 90% or even 100% of the garments.

Really spend some time analysing the fabrics that wear out quickly. It could be the composition, like a cheap cotton or polyester. Or perhaps it's the designer you bought the clothing from. Maybe the way they make the clothes, they aren't actually built to last? Or perhaps their sizing doesn't suit or fit you. These are the things you want to avoid choosing again.

If you don't know why you have never worn some of these pieces, perhaps you have a lack of knowledge about what actually suits you. It's important to understand which clothes work with your body shape, your lifestyle and your personality.

Understanding how you feel in your clothing is also important. Do you own clothing that makes you feel less attractive, beautiful and fantastic than you would like? What is the reason for this? If you are dressing to hide elements of your body shape you're uncomfortable with, this could be adding to the problem and not helping. Sometimes when people try to cover up their body it actually detracts from their appearance.

One of the biggest trends to hit our wardrobes has been the rise of casual wear. Casual can be fantastic. Leggings and activewear also have their place, however why not leave them to the purpose they were made for? And when you are done with your exercise, put them in the laundry and move on. Head to your wardrobe and find a casual outfit that allows you to move from meeting to family duties to a dinner at a restaurant with ease. More and more designers are creating clothing that can be multi-purpose and a lot more functional and at the same time stylish.

Perhaps get out some images of people you admire who have a stylish way of dressing during the day that you could interpret and replicate for yourself.

Revisit the oldies

Now for the pieces that you used to wear often and no longer do, but you just can't say goodbye to them. Take them all out. Again, lay them out so they are easily visible. Go through them one by one and ask yourself why you hold on to them. Are they sentimental items? Do you mind keeping them even if you don't wear them? If not, you can assess them and decide what to do. Ask yourself:

- Can I repair it?

- Can it be altered?

- Can it be reworked and made into something else?

- Can it be reworn, mended or reloved?

- Is there a way to have it recycled in my area?

You may also find you have become a little too routine with your clothing and would like to infuse some life into your wardrobe. For example, perhaps even though you feel comfortable in your clothes, you wear clothing that is more casual than you would like.

EXPERIMENT WITH NEW COMBINATIONS

Now it's time to grab a glass of vino or a spritz and play with the clothes you like and currently wear. The intention of this is to stretch your own relationship with fashion and expand your relationship with style.

Are there ways to fall in love again with what you currently own? See if you can find new clothing combinations. Ones that you haven't thought of before. This may require you to gain some knowledge around your body shape and dressing to accentuate your best features. If you already have this knowledge then set aside a few hours and get creative. Try new combinations, even if at first they seem like they won't work. You may be surprised. As you find new combinations, take some photos of them for reference and remember to wear them.

ORGANISE YOUR WARDROBE SO THAT IT INSPIRES YOU

One of the ways to maintain inspiration with your clothes at home is to organise your wardrobe so that it inspires you. It's great to organise your clothes into a system that suits your lifestyle and makes sense to the way you like to dress.

Start by looking at how your clothes are stored. Take some time to inspect each part — the drawers, the racks, the shoe section — and work out how to make them both beautiful and functional. One of the best things you can do is make sure all your coat hangers are the same. If you have coat hangers that are too big or irregular sizes, replace them with a slimline uniform selection so you can get maximum storage space in your wardrobe.

Next, it's good to make sure the clothes you wear the most are within easy reach. You can organise them into outfits or colours or by garment type; whatever works best for you. The main aim is to get them into order so that they are well cared for, visible and easily accessed in a way that makes sense for your lifestyle.

After this, organise the special-event outfits and clothing you wear less regularly in order of use. If you don't wear some items very often, is there somewhere else you can store them? It all depends on how much space you have available.

WHAT ITEMS CAN YOU REPAIR AND REUSE?

For the items that you have decided can be reworn, mended or reloved, choose a time by which you will have the clothes that need alterations done by, then put them in a bag or in your car immediately, ready to drop them off. The sooner you take them the sooner they can be put back into the working section of your wardrobe and worn again. Find ways to fall in love with your clothing over and over and over again. Relove the old to keep the need for new at bay.

With other items that need to be reloved, incorporate them back into your wardrobe in a way that you will remember to wear them with other outfits. Start wearing them as soon as possible. If you still don't feel comfortable in them, it's time to let them go. I don't mean sending them to the trash. Letting them go could mean asking who you know who may love to wear them: friends, relatives, or perhaps even finding Facebook groups dedicated to the resale of a specific designer, or to sharing clothes. If you don't know anyone, can you sell it online on a site such as eBay, or dedicated vintage sites, or take them to a local consignment store? (It will depend on the condition of each item.)

If there are clothes that really *are* at the end of their life, still don't put them in the bin or send them to landfill. See if you can find a way to give them to a textile waste recycler in your city, or perhaps even fashion brands that have a take-back system. Otherwise, how can you reuse them at home in other ways? As rags or cleaning items, for example.

We want to keep in mind the ethos of a circular economy, which is keeping clothes in use as long as possible. And when you no longer want to wear them, finding ways that they can be reloved, reworn or remade so that they stay in use longer.

* * *

Hopefully now you have a very clear picture of the clothes in your wardrobe. Understanding our fashion habits is the first step to a sustainable wardrobe. Once we know what we do well and what we can improve on, we are much better equipped to make new and exciting choices in the future. We have found a way to use and love more of what we have as well as a guide for how to shop so that new purchases will be a much better investment in the future. We have made a big step towards rethinking our fashion and creating better habits for the future.

CHAPTER 45

How to choose quality over quantity

'Elegance is elimination.' — Cristóbal Balenciaga

The quality of a garment is one thing that is sure to bring you satisfaction, provided you know what to look for. Knowing how to spot quality in a garment requires an understanding of the importance of fit, the fabrics, and the way it is sewn. Once you have the eye and appreciation for it, you never look back.

Quality doesn't always have to be expensive; it's more about knowing what to look for, which we will go through shortly. It's my wish that our approach to clothing be more like an investment than a discretionary item. When we care about what we own and love wearing each garment in our wardrobe then we are more likely to hold onto them. If we are going to turn the tide on fashion we need to rethink our relationship with it in this way. We can treasure every garment we own.

I'm going to go into detail about how to choose the right clothing and the benefits this gives us. For us to get the most mileage out of our clothing, we must adopt the approach of quality over quantity. It will not only ensure our clothes last longer, it will also guide us to choose well. It can take time to adjust our current wardrobe to this model, but it is worth it. You may already approach what you buy with consideration, and that is fantastic.

The term 'quality over quantity' has many elements. If you were to put two t-shirts side by side, at first glance they may seem identical, but when you take a closer look, it's the fabric type and composition as well as the construction that define how long each will last. These elements will determine your satisfaction level. It's all in the detail, and it is worthwhile paying attention when choosing your next garment.

WHAT IS QUALITY AND HOW DO WE SPOT IT?

When we decide to choose quality over quantity it may take more time to find the item we want but it is worth it. I encourage you to look at each garment as part of a whole. Like a piece of art in an art collection. By itself it stands alone as something beautiful, when you put the artwork in the context of the collection it also makes sense and compliments the other pieces. Now this doesn't mean you have to spend a fortune to find worthwhile pieces and we will cover that later in the book. At the same time it does mean that you hold a discerning eye when it comes to choosing clothing.

So, what is quality and how do we spot it? I could write a whole book just on the nature of quality. Overall, there are three things you can use to assess the quality of a garment:

- the fit

- the fabric

- the construction.

The quality of a garment is also relative to its purpose. If you expect a kimono to protect you from the wind and rain it will most definitely be hard to find the right item.

Let's have a closer look at these three issues.

Fit is everything

I was speaking with a friend recently; we both attended the same course at the Paris Fashion Institute, although years apart. She was saying that when she purchases a new dress or jacket for example, she always has the attitude that it will need some alterations. We spoke about how each person's body shape and proportions are so individual, it's not possible for a fashion brand to cater to all these variations. It was so great to hear her say this, because many people I talk to become dejected when they can't find something in a retail store just right for them. But it's not about their personal shape or size; it's that fashion brands have a very narrow definition of who they design for.

The way a garment fits on your body determines whether you are going to wear it again or not. Sometimes it's not always easy to pinpoint what is wrong with the fit but you just know that it doesn't feel 'right'. The fit is composed of the way the garment is designed. It's also made up of the amount of tailoring and shaping the item has. A kimono-style jacket is very different from a tailored coat. A basic kimono can be made up of as few as three pieces of fabric. Easily sewn together, it drapes around the body and doesn't require too much skill to make. A tailored jacket on the other hand has many pieces of fabric; it requires skill to design so that it fits the body well. It also requires skill to sew.

Each brand has their own sizing, meaning the proportions that they design their clothing to have. For example, from shoulders to the waist and hips, and from there to the ankle. At one end of the spectrum you have a couture garment which is made for the individual client. The body measurements are taken, and the pattern is made to fit perfectly. At the other end is a garment that has been designed to fit the basic shape of the body; a one-size-fits-all item.

When you buy a garment, first assess what type of garment it is, and then look at the way it should fit on the body. A t-shirt has a simple design. A dress can be very simple but it can also be intricate.

After considering the type of garment it is, you then need to know how the garment should fit for that specific item. When a garment fits you correctly it is neither too tight or too loose, unless the design is meant to be extra tight or voluminous. Details like pockets and button fastenings sit flat, and remain that way when you sit down. When you stand up, sit down and move about you can do so with ease, without feeling stress or pulling on the garment. When you raise your arms there is no pulling in the sleeve, and the shoulders should not raise high. If the garment scrunches up in the wrong places when you walk then the fit is also not right. If it gapes around the front neckline or lower back, the fit is not right (again, unless that is the design). The same applies if the fabric puffs up where it's not meant to, like at the back of the neck or our around the hips.

Whenever you can it's best to try on the garment. This way you are able to test the fit and quality before you buy it. When buying online there are a couple of ways to get around this. I recommend spending some time getting to know which designers and brands make clothing that best fits your body shape. Are you able to rely on their pieces being a consistent size? If so, you will be able to buy them online with confidence and you will want to keep them.

Another way to avoid sending items back is to get your measurements taken and have them as an easy reference for buying online. Brands should have at least the basic measurements for each size displayed with every garment on their website. If they don't then it can be a bit of a gamble. I know it seems like a bit of effort to get your measurements taken, but I promise it will serve you well.

The most important thing is to know the types of garments that work best for your body shape and height. If you don't then it can be easy to buy items that won't suit you and will make you look shorter, bigger, taller or smaller than you would like. If you already have an idea of what works for you then focus on fit and design so that an item shapes your body in the most elegant way possible.

Fabrics are the joie de vivre

Ah ... fabrics! They come in so many textures, colours, prints, weaves and knits! Fabrics are a world in themselves, and one of my favourite topics in fashion. I grew up around textural fabrics and yarns. My mother would spin her own yarn out of woollen fleece and then weave it on a loom. For me, the touch and appearance of a fabric can create a unique emotion.

Fabrics affect how we feel and how we respond to our clothing. They also influence the way we move about. Most importantly, the quality of a fabric determines how long your garment will last. This is why it's so important to get the fabric right. If the fabric tears or loses shape while we are wearing it, it's not a quality garment.

If you have even the most basic knowledge of what to look for you will be much better equipped to choose a quality garment. As I mentioned earlier when we asked the question about what our clothes are made of, there are many different scenarios behind every fabric. The more informed we are the better equipped we are to choose wisely. Please take the time to look on the resources section of my website (www.lalitalowe.com). You can also do your own research into different fabric types. Fabric knowledge across the globe is diminishing; most of the time people only know about simple compositions like cotton, wool or lycra, or a mix. There is so much more of a world of fabric knowledge to explore if you wish. It is truly amazing if you choose to open that door.

The first thing to do is to make sure a garment is made of an appropriate fabric for its purpose. You don't want to go hiking in chiffon, and it most likely wouldn't be functional or comfortable if your swimwear was made of wool. When touching and trying on a garment, think of what kind of activity you are going to do and if it suits.

Predominantly fabrics fall into two categories: woven and knit. Woven and knit fabrics perform in different ways and have a different structure. Woven fabrics usually don't have much stretch in them. Suits are generally made out of woven fabrics, and so is a basic cotton shirt. A knit fabric has more ability to stretch and shape to the body. When buying online, knit garments are easier to choose because of this stretch. Most activewear is made out of a knit fabric, so is swimwear, and – of course – knitwear.

The next thing to check is what the fabric is made of. There are natural fibres and manmade fibres. Hands down, my favourite – and what I always recommend to my clients – are natural fibres. Natural fibres breathe with the body, feel better to wear, and are biodegradable. (Another topic in itself, because the ability for a garment to decompose is a complex issue.) If you choose natural fibres of a good quality they can last for a long time; 5, 10, 15 years, or even more.

Then there are manmade fibres like polyester. The problem with these fibres is that they are toxic to the environment and the filaments wash into the water, creating issues. Polyester is basically plastic which is not good for humans, animals or the environment. Sometimes polyester has a place in garment use so we can't write it off.

If possible, my recommendation is to always choose natural fabrics. Natural fabrics are cotton, silk, wool and linen. However, just because it's a natural fabric doesn't mean it's good quality. The quality of cotton and wool is determined by the length of the fibres which are spun together. The longer the fibre, the stronger and more resilient the fabric will be. The length of the fibre in cotton and wool also determines the softness. Longer fibres for these two fabrics generally equals a higher quality. When choosing cotton, you want to make sure that it is soft. It will be higher quality and more pleasing to wear.

A woollen garment should be soft; the greater the softness the higher the yarn count. Merino wool is some of the softest in the world. Wool should not 'pill' easily, which is those little round balls that appear after a few wears. Pilling with a woollen garment does happen, but it should take time. The micron count of wool is significant: 21 micron is a standard quality, and if it's 19 or less you have a beautiful item. A micron is used as a measurement to determine the diameter of a wool fibre. The wool gets finer and softer as the micron measurement decreases. Merino wool is some of the finest and softest in the world, so when you are looking for a woollen garment try to make sure it is Merino.

Sadly, knowledge about different types of fabrics has diminished over the years. I encourage you to learn even a little bit about different fabrics, compositions and textures. There truly is a whole world out there. Even if you gather a small amount of knowledge about the basic types of fabric you wear in everyday clothing like cotton, wool, linen and silk, it will go a long way to helping you choose a quality fabric over a lesser one. It may also inspire you to learn more. Our experience of fashion is made so much richer when we understand fabrics.

How to assess the construction of an item

Have you heard the expression 'it came apart at the seams'? This is the perfect phrase to express what happens when a garment is poorly sewn.

The construction of a garment and the attention that goes into sewing it can help you spot quality.

First of all, when you are in a store you can check all the seams inside the garment. Make sure they are sewn evenly and have no puckering of stitches and fabric or gaps in the stitching. There should also be no loose threads.

The more neatly finished the seams of a garment are the more time has been taken to make it. And if there is lining covering up the inside of a jacket, for example, that is another element of quality. Next you can check all the 'pressure points' of a garment; for example, around the arm holes, the crotch area, and any fastenings like buttons or straps. You can make sure they are secure and well sewn by putting slight pressure and pulling against the seam to see whether it is sturdy or appears to be pulling easily. If the seams are slightly coming apart or shifting, you know it hasn't been made well.

* * *

Quality is everything. This includes the overall aesthetic of the garment. Whether it fits well and is a piece that will be relevant for years to come. Always buy the best you can afford. This doesn't mean expensive; it means the overall quality of the garment relative to the price. Choosing to buy less and buy better will ensure satisfaction for years to come. Being able to tell the quality of a garment will help you decide whether what you are being asked to pay is worthwhile or if there is a huge discrepancy between price and the actual garment. Over time you will develop a real eye for spotting quality.

CHAPTER 46

Understanding value

'You have to make choices based on your values — those are your personal ethics.' — Sass Brown

We don't value clothing as we used to. With so much choice and an unlimited amount of places to buy garments from, it's easy to forget the resources and energy it takes to create them. This is why we need to rethink our fashion.

As I spoke about earlier, our fashion values have been influenced — whether we realise it or not — by one hugely powerful segment of the industry, and that is fast fashion. Even if we don't like to buy from these brands, it has changed the culture around buying clothing. The expectations of price and how often things go on sale have changed dramatically. This in turn as decreased the amount we expect to pay for a garment overall. This change has also been influenced by globalisation and ecommerce.

Fashion has become so much more accessible, and like anything, when it becomes too easy to grasp we take it for granted. Clothing is everywhere, saturating our attention, which does not help when we are looking to buy new clothing because it can be hard to decipher the good from the bad. The quality from the disposable. It all gets lost in an ocean of fashion.

IT'S TIME TO REFOCUS AND RETHINK

So, what do we value? Does being able to buy something easily and quickly make it good? I would have thought that the anticipation of finding and investing in a piece of clothing that truly makes you look and feel your best is part of the joy of fashion. Real and lasting satisfaction does not come from a quick fix; this just propels desire which is never ending. In my opinion, restraint and simplicity are what create elegance. They bring about beauty. They give room for true appreciation.

It's so much easier to distract ourselves by looking for the next new thing. This is why we need to refocus and rethink the way we approach clothing. How do we do this? We orientate our appreciation back towards quality. We can do this by reminding ourselves of the value of a well-made garment. We have looked at all of these elements.

Doesn't the value of a garment also lie in the story behind it? When I was working in Paris in the workroom (or 'atelier' as it's called in France) of a fashion brand, I saw just how much effort goes into creating a fashion collection. It takes many skilled people to bring a well-thought-out collection to life and to create garments that people will love and want to invest in. I used to hear the head designer talk about her inspiration behind a collection, it could be a ballet she saw or an artist that had a particular type of brushstroke. It was this single moment of inspiration that set off the direction for everything that came after.

The next six months would involve a lot of collaboration, refinements and hard work. My favourite part was seeing and touching all the new beautiful fabrics that would come in from around France and other parts of the world. The atelier was a sea of activity and inspiration. Knowing how hard each person was working to bring that collection to life gave me a new appreciation of even a single garment created. Everybody was committed to making sure each garment fit the original vision and that it was made with precision and quality.

When we look at this experience in relation to the cost and value (they are *not* the same thing) of a garment, we can see there is so much that needs to be taken into consideration:

- The time it took to create the garment from beginning to the end.

- The quality of the fabrics.

- The well-thought-out design.

- A fantastic fit.

- Durability and elegance.

- The skill and workmanship of the person who created it.

- The inspiration and passion behind it.

- A garment that you will love and want to keep for many years.

- How fantastic it makes you look.

- Its wearability and functionality in your wardrobe.

- The pleasure of wearing it.

The next time you put on a garment or walk into a store to buy something new, have a think about just how much value and pleasure you can get from wearing that item. Let's rethink what value means to us, and make sure that any garment we buy in the future is carefully considered. Let's also revalue and relove the clothes we already own, so they bring us lots of pleasure in the future.

CHAPTER 47

Does all this mean I have to stop buying?

'It's about conscious consumption, not conspicuous consumption.' — Bandana Tewari

NO ... IT DOESN'T

Of course, I am not saying you have to stop buying. We all need to keep our look fresh and relevant. And who doesn't love the joy of a gorgeous new piece that was made with your name on it? What I am saying is that we need to rethink what we buy and we need to be more considered.

Rethinking what we buy involves assessing our fashion in terms of the story we want to tell. Rather than just buying clothes on a whim, why not focus on carving out a really unique and personal style? You will be so happy wearing the pieces in your wardrobe that it will be more about *what* you have than *how much* you have.

If we focus on finding the right clothes — whether it means taking longer than expected or aborting a shopping mission because we didn't find the right piece — then we can build a collection of clothing that will satisfy for years to come. And before even thinking about buying something new, I recommend getting your current wardrobe to a place where you truly love what you have in there (as we looked at earlier).

To stop buying clothing altogether is like an insult to a woman's or a man's personal style, because the injection of a new sweater or a new pair of pants can change our entire look. It can breathe fresh air into our wardrobes. But how about it be one or two pieces in a year instead of a monthly event? How does that feel? Always question the purpose of a garment in your wardrobe. Tighten the reigns on shopping and direct your purchases with a mindful eye. This mindful approach will bring you a well-curated wardrobe of wonderful pieces that truly satisfy.

To think in a sustainable way, before buying anything new remember the criteria we have covered in this book. Any new garment that comes into your life must have a purpose. It also needs to have longevity. Will it still be in your wardrobe in 15 to 20 years? That is the hallmark of a worthy piece. If we think in terms of longevity and quality for our entire wardrobe, it changes the way we approach fashion entirely.

CHAPTER 48

Exploring vintage fashion

'Vintage is now as much a part of fashion as anything else.'
— Bay Garnett

Wearing and shopping for vintage fashion has become a respected part of a person's wardrobe in recent years. These days vintage fashion covers everything from a handmade bolero of the 1940s to a preloved Stella McCartney blazer from last season. The definition is wide and the wonderful gems you can find are endless.

The original definition of a vintage garment was a piece approximately 20 years old or more. It was a collectible piece, and sometimes an iconic garment from a designer's range. My definition of vintage, and the new approach to this area of clothing, is a little broader. I see a vintage garment as one that is preloved and being resold by someone who owned the garment originally.

There is a vast reservoir of high-quality clothing already out there which has been worn before and is now looking for a new owner. This is a way to inject new (to you) items into your collection without placing a burden on the planet. Shopping for vintage pieces is one of my favourite ways to find a coveted garment that I am either not able to afford otherwise or have missed out on. It also opens up the door to finding specific garments that are not trending at the moment but would look very relevant in your wardrobe. Imagine for example if you looked best in straight-leg high-waisted pants but nobody was making them right now? Vintage shopping is the way to go in this situation.

WHERE DO I BUY VINTAGE ITEMS?

So, where do you go to find these amazing pieces? There are many websites which specialise in selective areas of vintage clothing. Some only sell true 1940s and 1950s clothing, and if you keep your eye on these sites over a period of time, you can find incredible pieces like a Balenciaga classic evening dress, for example.

There are also some very reputable websites that sell authenticated and preowned luxury fashion. If you are looking for designer pieces, you want to make sure they have been authenticated and these websites have systems in place to do so. Why is a luxury resale site a great option? Not because it is luxury, but because you are able to buy quality, well-made garments.

If you are looking for something more local, there are often resale and consignment stores which curate well-made pieces. If you are looking to get a little more creative then your local thrift store is a fantastic place to explore.

I have also seen many stores on Instagram where people are curating vintage pieces with a specific slant, like wispy lace dresses or colourful '60s summer pieces. It really is getting very specific. These sellers often only sell on Instagram, and you need to set up alerts for when new pieces become available because they sell out quickly. They are usually contactable with a direct message or an email but have no website. When shopping on a website or in an app like Instagram, always follow the tips in the next chapter for online shopping. They will guide you so you make the right choices that fit you properly so there will be no disappointments.

Some of my favourite places to shop for vintage are the luxury resale sites. There really are some great gems to be found, and these garments are often well looked after with many in immaculate condition. When I was living in Paris, I had my eye on some amazing Gucci wedges of the current collection but never bought them. A year later I kept my eye on one of the vintage sites, and within a few weeks found them in immaculate condition in the size I was after.

I recommend vintage pieces that meet a set of criteria. They must be in near-perfect condition and have been treated with care. They should be appropriate for your personal fashion strategy and be a quality item. If it's a silk blouse from Chanel from five years ago, well that is an investment and a piece that will serve you for many years. It may also be a piece from a little-known designer where the workmanship is impeccable. An old synthetic piece from a fast-fashion brand won't cut it.

FINDING THE RIGHT ITEMS FOR YOU

I love to talk about vintage because I know just how satisfying the right garments can be. Here are me seven key tips to make sure you find the right items.

Sign up for alerts

Some vintage sites allow you to sign up for alerts for specific designers or types of garments. Signing up for alerts is awesome if you are looking for a particular item; for example, an iconic Yves Saint Laurent le smoking jacket. You will be among the first to know when it comes online and therefore more likely to purchase it.

Buy with the end in mind

The key to buying anything is to buy with a purpose. To have an overall strategy for your fashion collection. Know the types of pieces you need. The ones that you will wear for years to come. They could be signature items like a jacket or blazer that will take a range of outfits from average to wow.

Always ask questions

Never buy a garment you are unsure about for any reason. If details are missing in the description of the listing, make sure to contact the seller to ask more questions. If you are unsure of the fit, fabric, quality or anything else, asking questions is a must. If the seller is dismissive or fails to answer your question clearly, it's best to move on.

Buy only from verified vintage sellers

We all know about the lucrative market for fake items. These days it can be hard to tell a fake from the real thing. To avoid buying a dud, make sure to shop only with verified luxury resellers who test the authenticity of an item before putting it on their site.

Know your budget

There is no point buying vintage if you spend more than you can afford. Knowing your budget also means being aware of what a garment is worth on the market and knowing how much it should sell for as a vintage item. Always go for a fair price. This price will be either what you are willing to pay, what it should sell for depending on its condition, or what the market value is now.

Inspect the images to assess quality

Always inspect the images carefully. Most sites have a 'zoom' function which will allow you to see the quality of the fabric. Make sure there is no pilling, holes or scuffs. Check shoes to make sure there is no damage to the leather or material. Check clothing for any signs of wear and tear. If there is too much damage to the item, likely it will be left unworn when you receive it.

* * *

Finding vintage pieces can be equally satisfying, if not moreso, than buying new clothing because you can source pieces that are in line with your style. You can also take your time to find the perfect pieces. If you buy well they will be an investment you can wear for years to come. Buying clothing in this way is a sustainable approach to fashion.

CHAPTER 49

Navigating virtual purchases

'Only buy clothes that you plan to keep forever.
It's important to see trends for what they are: a game.'
— Carine Roitfeld

Increasingly, people prefer to buy clothing online over shopping instore. There are more options to find the size and colour you are after, you can cross-reference brands, and choose exactly the right piece for you. The world is really your oyster when it comes to ecommerce.

But buying clothing online is not as straightforward as you might think. And I find many women that I talk to have had their fair share of returns. Returns are a time waster and a money waster. It usually costs extra to send the item back, and nobody wants to have to expend that extra energy. I'm sure you also want to be able to put the item on and wear it as soon as you receive it, rather than having to send it back.

HOW TO ENSURE A SUCCESSFUL ONLINE PURCHASE

Unfortunately, fashion retail in the virtual space is also creating a huge environmental problem, with huge volumes of carbon emissions being created in transportation and packaging. As I mentioned earlier in the book, returns are usually disposed of in landfill or incinerated as clothes are sent back on a daily basis. So how can we do our part to minimise our impact? Let's look at some of the things you can do to ensure a success-ful online purchase and minimise returns.

Know your measurements

The key to buying anything online is to know your measurements. It's best to have someone take them professionally. This includes your height, waist, hip and bust/chest measurements. A garment description on a website should always have a size chart available in the listing. You usually have to click on a small amount of text saying 'size chart' or similar to view the measurements for each size.

Each brand has different sizing; you may have noticed that you can be a size 8 in one brand and a size 10 in another. This is why it's so important to check your measurements against each garment to find the best fit.

Know that it will suit your body shape

Knowing how to dress to suit your unique proportions and body shape is an essential element of personal style. Buying the wrong garment for your body shape is the reason you feel self-conscious and uncomfortable when you wear it. It's also one of the main reasons clothing remains unworn or gets thrown out. Knowing your body shape is also key to finding the pieces that make you feel attractive and confident. If in doubt about what suits you, make sure to get some professional advice.

Check your fabrics

I touched on fabrics earlier and how they perform differently on the body. Overall you will have two types of fabrics to choose from: knits and wovens. Knits will stretch and have more room to mould on the body if the sizing of the garment isn't the right fit. Knit fabrics are used in activewear, leggings, polos, t-shirts and lots of other casual wear.

Then you have the wovens — silks, wool, organza, twill and suiting. For example, your regular corporate wear is most likely made of a woven, as are suits and shirts. Make sure to check the fabric to know how much room you will have for error when you buy it.

Do you really need it?

Browsing online can be a fun experience; there are so many beautiful garments to compare, and once you find the ones you like there is also the rush of satisfaction and anticipation. However, at the end of the day, do you really need that extra t-shirt or dress or pair of pants? Buyer's remorse is a real thing and very often leads to a return.

Is it sustainable and ethical?

Take a deep dive into the website you are looking at buying from. Is there a dedicated section on sustainability? Are they telling you their targets to reduce their impact? Is it clearly communicated that their fabrics are sourced sustainably? Can they show you where their factories are and how their workers are treated? These are all things that should become a first point of reference if you are wanting to make better buying decisions. So remember to be really aware when you are navigating a website. Commit to buying from people who share their passionate vision for change in every section of their business.

When in doubt, don't

Do you absolutely love the item you are looking at and will you wear it? My number one saying has always been, if you ever find yourself doubting, even for a minute, walk away. It's very often that people put things in their shopping carts and leave them. Why is that? Because of doubt and a lack of strategy. Giving yourself time to decide is like a breath of fresh air. Once you have walked away or closed the screen or shopping app, make a conscious decision to think about the purchase and how it fits into your collection. If it doesn't and you can't see yourself wearing it for many years to come, with multiple outfits, walk away.

* * *

Buying online has many benefits but also many drawbacks. The main thing is to have a clear intention for what you are looking for. Know your size and know your values when it comes to sustainability. Make buying online work for you and be a way to give back to a designer or community that will benefit greatly — then your online purchase will be beneficial on so many levels.

CHAPTER 50

How to budget for your fashion

'Every time you shop, always think, 'Will I wear this a minimum of 30 times?' — Livia Firth

Do you know how much you spend on clothes each year? Most of us have no idea. Should we? It's possible you don't even need a budget. If you've decided you will have quality pieces over quantity, this means that in time you will be buying fewer pieces. However, depending on what you buy and how often, it can be good to do some planning in advance.

Any time we review our finances we take a moment or two to reflect on how much we've earned as well as how much we've spent. Spending too much is always a concern, as is not generating enough income. My question is, have you ever included your clothing as part of your annual budget? And, I guess, an even bigger question is, should you?

What we wear can have a significant impact on our life, though this impact may not seem obvious. However, when we understand the relationship between what we wear and how it makes us feel, as well as the effect it has on our work opportunities, dating life and of course personal branding, the impact becomes clear.

Most financial experts are of the same mind when it comes to spending money on clothes. They say that you should spend around 5% of your budget or 5% of your personal income after tax on clothing a year. What does that actually look like? Well, if you take home $60,000 a year after tax, you could spend $3000 a year on clothes or $250 a month. Of course, this is just a number, and for you it may seem too high or too low; the main thing is to realistically assess what you can afford to spend on your clothes each year and stick to it. Your personal fashion budget includes more than just new items; it also includes alterations and reshaping garments as well as any costs for dyeing.

SETTING YOUR BUDGET

There are two elements to consider when it comes to setting your fashion budget. One is to work out what clothes you need to buy over a calendar year, and the other is to understand what value you are getting from the clothes you purchase. I'll talk about both of these a little more throughout the chapter. Having a clothing budget does not mean working out the clothes you need to buy and setting an amount accordingly; it's actually the reverse. Decide the percentage of your income you have available to spend on clothes and then choose your purchases wisely to ensure value for money.

Looking at your fashion purchases as an investment as opposed to an expense is a good place to start when deciding where to allocate your fashion budget. When we look at the price of a garment, we need to factor in the true cost as well as the monetary cost. The true cost includes all that we have spoken about in terms of environmental and humanitarian impacts. These issues are a big part of deciding whether or not to purchase an item.

We also need to work out how often we will wear this item over its lifetime, and divide the purchase price by this figure to get your 'pay per wear' figure. This tends to highlight the perceived value we get from lower cost (and lower quality) items as opposed to the actual value we get from higher quality (and higher cost) items.

Imagine you see a stunning blue blazer in a store that costs $2500. You put it on, and it fits like a glove. The only other blazer you have at home is slightly baggy around the shoulders, the hem is too long for your height, and you haven't worn it as often as you thought. You just don't feel that confident wearing it, so you don't wear it; it's reached its use-by date. And while you can also have this item altered, you have considered buying a new item for some time so the investment needs to be factored in.

So, the new blazer is $2500, a considerable investment. But if you are wearing it three times a week for 45 weeks of the year, and assuming that it should last and be in style for eight years because it is a high-quality, classic item, over the life of the jacket you will wear it approximately 135 times. The price of the blazer, when looking at it from a 'pay per wear' price, is $18 per wear.

Now, that is value if you think about the way you will feel when wearing the blazer, the impact it will have on your professional image and brand, and the length of time you get to wear it. If you bought a cheap $250 blazer you would have to replace it in a couple of years, the attention to detail (which affects the overall look) would be much less appealing, plus there is more likelihood of fallen hems, holes, fading and pilling in the first year. Consider, how many times will you wear it and feel your best in it?

I use this approach of 'pay per wear' with many garments I choose, and I base my buying decisions on the following factors:

1.   The quality of the fabric.

2.   How well the garment fits.

3.   The quality of the finishings, including buttons, hems and pockets.

4.   The quality of design and whether it's a style that will last more than one season – preferably at least a few years.

Think about value for money as well as its environmental and humanitarian cost when purchasing a new garment for your wardrobe. Buying cheaper items that don't last as long or look their best after a short amount of time is simply false economy. It pays to have fewer garments that speak volumes in terms of quality. Your self-esteem, personal brand and professional image will thank you for it. And you'll be surprised by just how many people notice the quality of the clothing you wear.

CHAPTER 51

Wearing it more than once

'Why don't you ... find one dress that you like and have it copied many times? You will be much more successful than if you try to produce the same effects each evening.'
— Diana Vreeland

I don't know about you, but when I find something I like I buy it in multiple colours. I have a favourite light-grey sweater that I knew instantly would suit me when I saw it online. It was totally me. I ordered it straight away, and within a few days it was on my doorstep. What a gorgeous piece, hand-knitted in the front and machine-knitted in the sleeves to create a stunning texture and volume. After I had been wearing it for a while I realised it was a piece I would want to wear forever. So I went back online to find it in black, and luckily I was able to source one. I wear these sweaters regularly.

How do you feel about wearing a garment more than once? Are you someone who needs to be seen in a different outfit all the time? If you have a public profile it may be challenging to wear something more than once. Unfortunately, this especially applies to women because we get judged by what we wear every day. Not that it should be that way, but it does happen. Men on the other hand have a much easier job. They can get away with wearing the same suit many times over.

We need to challenge this ideal. It's not economical or practical to only wear a garment once, nor does it fit into a sustainable approach. Fast fashion has contributed to this problem when people started to feel it was easier to throw away a garment and buy a new one than wear it again. Fast fashion has perpetuated a disposable culture.

STYLE REPEATS

Arianna Huffington started a movement to change the stigma around wearing a garment more than once. This applies especially for celebrities and people in the media, who are scrutinised and watched closely with every outfit. This especially applies for women, and Arianna Huffington wants to change this. She coined the phrase 'style repeats' to encourage women to wear the clothes they love more often. She said that men can wear the same item more than once, so why not women?

This approach is now becoming more accepted, especially when you see people like Kate Middleton from the Royal Family deliberately wearing an outfit a second or third time. And there are many other celebrities who have been getting on board with this movement.

In 2019 Jane Fonda took a stance when she decided she would never buy a new garment ever again. At the Oscars in 2020 she wore a burgundy evening dress encrusted with Swarovski crystals, a dress she had worn previously to a red carpet event at the 2014 Cannes Film Festival. For a woman with a profile such as Jane Fonda, this was a big step to take, considering the criticism and pressure celebrities face to always wear something new. This was a deliberate statement, and it is one we can all take to heart. With women like Jane Fonda and Arianna Huffington leading the way, why can't we embrace wearing our clothes more than once, and perhaps many, many times?

Entrepreneurs and great minds have also said that repeating an outfit, and even taking it a step further to wear a kind of uniform each day, takes the fuss out of life and helps them focus on what matters most — their work, their passion. Steve Jobs was known for his black turtleneck sweater, and designer Carolina Herrera is known for her signature look of a white shirt worn with skirts.

Why not challenge yourself to wear your clothes more often? You can find ways to accessorise them and mix them with other clothes in different combinations. This will go a long way to creating a more sustainable approach to fashion. It may also surprise you the multiple styling options you come up with.

CHAPTER 52

What a personal collection is and why you need one

'Building a wardrobe is like building a circle of friends your whole life.' — Diane Von Furstenberg

Earlier on I mentioned the value of seeing the clothes in your wardrobe like an art collection. I say this not to intimidate you or make you think you have to buy only expensive clothes. I say this to introduce the idea of having a carefully selected set of clothes that complement each other. This purposeful assemblage saves us time, can fulfil our fashion needs, and contribute towards a sustainable style. An art collection tells a story. It reveals personality, history, contemporary life, relevance. Our clothes can do this also.

There's a big difference between having clothes just for the sake of functionality or as a representation and strategic communication of who you are. A personal collection is deliberately put together. Each item has a purpose. A piece of art has relevance and beauty on its own, and at the same time when you view it in the context of a collection, in a gallery or your wardrobe, it has a bigger purpose and fits in with the whole.

Functional clothes are everywhere: white shirts, black pants, cashmere sweaters. But when you train yourself to look for more detail in clothing, a functional piece can be turned into an elevated basic. It may be that the sleeve has a lightly different shape or the collar is cut so it moulds around the neckline. It could be a simple black skirt is not so simple at all, that it has a fabulous embossed matt texture. These slight variations start to build a refined and magnificent collection. Weave in these pieces with some classic garments and it has body and substance. On top of these elevated basics and classic pieces, you can then add in your pop of colour and your statement pieces. The ones that say bam! *This is me!*

ALL ABOUT YOU

Each of us is unique, and the beauty of a personal collection is that it's all about you and its relevance to your lifestyle. Take Iris Apfel for example, an American businesswoman, interior designer, and fashion icon. Her bold, colourful and playful style is apparent in every garment. It is a collection representative of her, and she has made it work. It suits her personality as well as the point she is at in her life. She takes print, colours and volume to the limit. Iris Apfel's statement is 'more is more', which works for her because she uses each piece and it all plays a part in her definite style.

Having a personal collection fits in with a sustainable outlook because each piece is bought consciously. Of course there are times when you set flight to the wind and buy something not in your plan. But as you build your collection, you will find that your eye gets trained to look for specific shapes and colours. So a whimsical purchase may not be so whimsical but more of a perfect opportunity seized in the moment.

One of my favourite style icons is Carine Roitfeld. She is the former editor-in-chief of *Vogue Paris*, and now has her own magazine *CR Fashion Book*. Carine's style is very much the epitome of the mysterious and sexy French woman. She wears timeless pieces, sometimes with an edge. Her personal style of a pencil skirt, slinky silk blouse, elegant heels and sometimes a dash of leopard print is iconic. This look is also perfect for her body shape as well as her height. She wears this look in many fabrics, prints and combinations, and it is most definitely her signature, recognisable look. Carine Roitfeld also believes in pieces that you will wear forever.

Overall, discretion and restraint are two values that will take you a long way to building a beautiful collection of clothes. They will guide you to take time when choosing each piece. This direction of a more sustainable wardrobe means making better buying decisions and only when they truly fit in with your overall story. Remember, an art collection tells a story, your story. It must be love when you buy it, or wear it, or don't.

CHAPTER 53

Protecting your investment

'Carefully choose the clothes you wear and take the time to care for them with love.' — Stella McCartney

Now that we are investing in more quality items and committed to keeping them for longer, it makes sense to protect your investment. You have invested time to research the most appropriate clothing, and perhaps made more of a financial investment. With all this in mind there are steps you can take to ensure these beautiful pieces last as long as possible.

In this book we are talking about a sustainable approach to fashion as an outlook and a way of life. That each piece we own has been chosen with consideration for people and the planet as well as our own personal aesthetic. When we choose quality pieces, taking care of them will ensure they really can last forever. Friends of mine have pieces in their wardrobe they bought 20, 30 or 40 years ago which are still going strong. This is so different to the fast fashion mentality. It is a positive approach that needs to be revisited if we are to change the momentum of the industry.

MAKING SURE YOUR CLOTHES WILL LAST

So how do we make sure our clothes will last? If you look into the word 'sustainability', it contains the answer within itself and gives us the direction. The word 'sustain' means to maintain, preserve, keep alive, bolster and nourish. These words show us how we can take care of our investment and keep our valued pieces around for as long as possible. Maintaining our garments in the right way also preserves our enjoyment of them. There are many ways to do this. We can store them with care, use the right washing conditions, mend, repair and use alterations to keep our clothes alive. When a stain or hole appears, if we get onto the task as soon as its needed there may be no evidence there was ever an issue.

The opposite also applies, which is what happened to a cashmere sweater I had bought overseas. It was a classic piece that I would wear all the time, and of course with frequent use it started to wear. One day, a small hole appeared, and what did I do? Nothing. I kept thinking I would get to it later. But later never came; the hole became bigger and bigger. It's not irreparable, but it will take more skill and money to have it repaired and will most likely be visible afterwards. Still, repairing even at this stage is much better than disposing of it.

Repairs

Let's start with repair; this is a task that derails many wardrobes and sends a lot of items to landfill.

One way to prolong the life of our clothes is by making friends with a local tailor or seamstress. Not any seamstress, because they are not all created equal. Some are fantastic at minor tasks like buttons and hems, but anything greater than that is a stretch. So I suggest asking friends or colleagues who also care about their clothes for recommendations. Even a staff member at a local boutique should be able to put you onto someone worthwhile. Try to find a person who is a trained tailor or dressmaker because then they will be able to do more detailed and skilled alterations.

What can you repair? More often than not a damaged item can be rescued. So, take it in as soon as possible. When an issue arises, tuck the item into a lovely bag and put it in your car so you will drop it off the next time you are out and about. You can even put a reminder in the calendar on your phone.

Alterations

Another tip for longevity when it comes to our personal collection is reworking garments with alterations. There is so much that can be done, especially with vintage pieces that you feel are outdated. So when you are considering throwing an item out, or sending it to a seconds store, why not reimagine it?

Remember that dress you wore 20 years ago, the one with the shoulder pads? The one you kept because of the sentiment connecting to a time and place? How can you rework it to become something new? The shoulder pads could go to begin with, and then perhaps the hemline can be taken up or let out or the sleeves rearranged.

It's possible to change the length and width of sleeves as well as the shoulders of a top, jacket or dress. You can also make legs of pants and jeans slimmer. The waist of an item can be taken in, and sometimes let out. You can add embellishments like beading or trims to add new life. There is also the option to have garments dyed, although finding a non-toxic dye company may be a little harder. Even if you can't yet see what is possible for an unloved or unworn item in your wardrobe, take it to your newfound best friend, the alterations extraordinaire, and ask their advice. You may be amazed at the possibilities.

When is an item worth reworking? This depends on the type of garment and the amount of work needed. A quality suit may be costly but can also provide many more years of pleasure if updated. This goes for any item that has been well made and you have already had a lot of pleasure wearing. The items you fell out of love with quickly may only require some simple reshaping. If you assess the worth of the garment and the investment needed and the amount of work required, you will have your decision.

Washing and drying

The everyday washing and drying of our clothes has an impact on how long they last. Washing machines wear down the fibres in our clothes over time. The cycle and the types of laundry wash we use also make a difference.

In this age of convenience many clothes are made to be machine washable, however when we are choosing quality items our approach needs to be a little more considered if we truly want to take care of and prolong the life of our clothes. Always take note of the washing instructions on the care label, but at the same time act with caution. Natural fibres especially have different ways of responding to washing, so it's best to do some research on each new garment when you buy it. Find out about how to take care of each type of fabric. I know it seems like an effort and a bit of a bore, however this extra attention will provide a lot of pleasure in the long run. Your clothes will retain their fibre integrity, their colour and shape, and for a greater amount of time.

I know hand washing takes time. But please for a minute just hear me out when I say that some of your clothes will be much better off, especially those made of natural fibres. Woollens in particular are very delicate; as soon as any rubbing action takes place it changes their integrity. This action matts and felts the fibres and can make them shrink. So the best thing is to hand wash in luke warm water without wringing or pushing and pulling. Gently soak and move the item about in the water; press the water out and then put in a towel, gently pressing again to remove excess water. Drying flat in the shade afterwards is a must.

Do not leave your clothing in a washing basket for too long. When clothing is dirty it's the perspiration that has the most damaging effect, as well as been crumpled in a heap in the basket or − worse − on the floor. So try to wash your clothes as soon as you can.

Environmentally our washing machines create a huge carbon imprint as well as a demand on water resources. So being economical as best you can contributes to a sustainable approach.

And then there is the dryer − it has the most impact of all. The extreme heat and the movement of the dryer create a lot of wear and tear. If you need to use a dryer, do so sparingly. You can think ahead a little and wash your clothes a few days in advance if needed for a specific event. Line drying, especially in the sun, is antibacterial, killing nasties, and it also leaves the fresh, crisp and pure scent of cleanliness.

Stains

Last but not least are stains: tomatoes, wine, oil ... you name it. The best thing to do is act quickly. I recommend investing in a book that covers removal of stains of all types, and if not, use Dr Google. When you have a stain, do not let the garment dry after you have treated it because it will become much harder to remove. Know that it can often take more than one attempt before a stain will come out.

Gently attend to the stain without damaging the fabric. If truly in doubt about how to treat it or if it's a delicate item, take it straight away or the next business day to a reputable dry cleaner and do not treat it beforehand.

Storage

Storing our clothes in the right way is an art. The wrong hanger can stretch and distort an item, and if it is not meant to have a hanger at all it can create irreparable damage. I know it's easier said than done. Throwing clothes on a chair and leaving them there for a few days may feel harmless — and quite frankly, satisfying on those weeks when you are exhausted. However, our clothes can stretch, they can catch and get worn in all kinds of ways.

There is also something satisfying about having clothes hung with order and care, about drawers that make it easy to select something each time you open them. I remember my girlfriend in New York used to fold all her pieces so delicately, just like her nature, and this gentleness and order inspired me to do the same. The joyful art of packing and storing our clothing was made attractive by Marie Kondo. If you haven't seen her TV series I recommend it; she has a lot of wonderful tips and tricks for folding clothes and storing them in the most beautiful ways.

So I encourage you, just like with washing and drying, to follow the care label for any storage recommendations your clothes may have. Use Dr Google to research how different fibres respond to hanging and packing, and practise taking your wardrobe organisation to a new level. Your clothes will love you for it and they will last much longer also.

Plan ahead

Have you ever had a moment when you go out for dinner and it starts to rain just as you arrive at the restaurant? Or perhaps it's really hot and you arrive at your destination needing a change of clothes. Planning ahead for these moments can be a wardrobe lifesaver. Your stunning suit, beautiful new dress, or flash new shoes could go from a cleanly pressed immaculate look to dishevelled drunk in a snap. Some ways to avert this are:

- Look at the weather in advance and wear appropriate gear.

- Have a change of clothes available.

- Take an appropriate weather-friendly coat.

- Keep a spare pair of stylish walking shoes in the car or a carry bag to get you from A to B.

- Have an umbrella in the car.

- Book a driver for a function and avoid the fuss.

Then there are the times when you are going from meeting to meeting but you need a pair of walking shoes in between; don't feel embarrassed about taking them with you. You can slip them on as you are moving from one place to another, and find a discreet place to change before you enter the next meeting, function or event.

Travel

So many mishaps can happen when we travel. It's easy for clothes to get ruined in transit. Perhaps a splashed coffee down the front of your white shirt as the stewardess on the plane hands it to you. Or maybe you reach down to pick up some luggage and the sleeve on your jacket rips. Even worse, you send an important and favourite item to the hotel laundry and it comes back destroyed. How can you protect your clothes and prepare for such events?

Firstly, it's always good to take a change of clothes in your carry-on luggage, especially if you are travelling for business. If your outfit gets damaged you will have peace of mind that you have something else to wear. Next, it's important to attend to the issue as soon as you can. If you have a ripped shirt, take it off and repair it or get it to an alterations specialist immediately. And when you're travelling it's great to have a mending kit with you and — if you're not very good on the sewing front — a few links to repair videos on YouTube.

* * *

All in all, taking care of our clothes is part of a strategy. We are aligning with a much bigger purpose. Investing in our clothes is investing in the future of this planet. Each of our actions counts, right down to the mending of a t-shirt. We are cultivating a sustainable mindset that can be applied across the board.

CHAPTER 54

Embrace your aesthetic

'There's no how-to roadmap to style. It's about self expression and, above all, attitude.' — Iris Apfel

Aesthetics can be defined as a set of principles concerned with the nature and appreciation of beauty. I just love this word because it captures the essence of enjoying the things that bring you joy. It is a state of appreciation and the recognition of beauty.

When it comes to personal style, I find the word 'aesthetic' is a great way to take us out of the idea of there being one way to do something, that style is a formula. We are all unique. Our body shape, eye colour, skin tone — no combination is the same. Add in our personality and lifestyle and it's a story waiting to be told. But how do you tell that story and what are you trying to say?

WHAT LIGHTS YOU UP?

What is it about fashion that lights you up? Perhaps you love jackets and invest in them as you see fit. Is it a jacquard print that takes your breath away? Or perhaps you love a classic cut suit with a twist like a unique printed lining. Each of us has our own personal aesthetic. Fashion is self-expression. It's personality wrapped in up in a garment.

Your personal aesthetic, or style as some like to call it, is something that could be defined by a particular mixture of elements. When we talk about personal style it used to be defined as classic or elegant or preppy or bohemian, and many more. These days personal style seems to incorporate more individual elements than before. It's so helpful though to know what your overall preferences towards fashion are. To be able to identify what your aesthetic and style is so that you can embrace it fully.

STATEMENT PIECES

One you have established your basic style and redefined your wardrobe, it's time to think about those pieces that will bring wow to any outfit. I like to call these 'statement pieces'.

Just say you have a collection of bold print dresses and this is your style, a well-designed black coat or jacket may be a statement piece. It could be something you can wear over any of those dresses to change the tone or message of the look you usually wear. I have a gorgeous jacket with metal beadwork down the front that is definitely a statement piece. I just adore it so much; it's a bold piece and I don't wear it often, however it can be worn as an event piece but also during the day if it's dress down with jeans and a t-shirt and trainers. The base of my wardrobe is mostly neutrals, so to add in a piece like this brings extra personality to any outfit.

Statement pieces can also be simple items of a different texture to your outfit, like a chiffon blouse that will take any skirt or pair of pants you wear to another level. They may have more detail or less detail, depending again on the base of your wardrobe.

CULTURAL PIECES

Included in these statement pieces are cultural pieces. Those garments that connect you with your tradition and heritage. How can you incorporate them into your look? It's so great to be able to add pieces from your own culture to your outfits, especially in Western cultures where our clothes are very much homogenised. These items will connect you to your roots; they are your uniqueness and style.

When I first started living in Paris, working in the fashion industry, one of my girlfriends who was also new to the city thought she had nothing to wear. When it came time for fashion week she only had a small selection of clothes to choose from. She asked me what to do.

Worried about not looking good enough or appropriate for the fashion crowd, I assured her she would be fine. Each time I had met her after work she was always dressed so elegantly. It didn't matter what she wore, she looked the part. For one important event she told me about one traditional piece from Mexico, a white bolero that she was thinking about wearing with some basic black pants and a shirt.

She was worried it wouldn't work, or that it wouldn't look good enough to present professionally and fashionably among her luxury fashion peers. Sending me a picture before the event, I assured her it looked fantastic. My girlfriend decided she would wear it, and on the day she looked suitably fantastic. When she was asked to pose in a photo for the press it was another confirmation. This moment illustrated to me the power of having a few items well chosen and thought out and an intricate cultural piece to top it off.

Are there a particular garments you currently have that would work? If not, do some research to find them from a relative, your grandmother or grandfather, or some vintage sites. Alternatively you could have them made by someone in your community or a local artisan. If you are living away from your native country, shopping online, taking a trip or connecting with people who you know there are all ways to find those unique pieces from your heritage.

So remember, your personal aesthetic is a representation who you are. Your clothing is a part of this. Why not make it the best it can be by incorporating well-curated pieces along with signature and cultural pieces that tell us who you are. It can make up a very unique selection of clothing.

Most of all, you want to love what you wear, because isn't that where the joy and pleasure of fashion lies? Knowing how to encapsulate your style in a few key elements and elevate them to the next level will create a winning wardrobe. Embrace who you are.

PART VII

What the world of fashion could look like

'A new frontier beckons,
demanding that we reinvent
everything from scratch.'

—Li Edelkoort

HERE WE ARE. We've come a long way and we've learnt so much. So what will the world of fashion look like if we rethink it? This is where we take a look at the future of the industry and our wardrobes. We look at what is already being done and how it will continue as we start asking more questions.

The future of fashion is hopeful; we all play a part as individuals, consumers and governments, and the following chapters examine what this could look like. A lot of these are global trends and they are already taking place. This means we are on the right path.

As we return to a more considered approach with our fashion and start to look on our very own doorsteps, there are many ways our actions can have an impact. It's going to require a shift in thinking and an adjustment in the way we approach fashion, but the outcome can be great. We will have much more inspiring and satisfying wardrobes. Our commitment to a refined set of values will have a positive influence in ways you may not be able to see right now.

There is a long way to go and we need to be patient. However, the transformation has begun, and that's what we need to set our sights on.

CHAPTER 55

Going local

'We develop skills, provide jobs and stay connected with everyone who works with our product.' — Bianca Spender

Buying locally will become more and more important in the future as we bring our focus to reducing our carbon footprint. As well as the environmental benefits, a culture thrives when art and creativity are celebrated. Through buying locally we support the creativity of local designers, growers and makers, adding to a richer experience for the community overall.

There is a sense of belonging, contribution and pride walking out of a local boutique with a purchase you adore. If the boutique is in the local neighbourhood, it's easy to find yourself stopping by every now and then just to see what's in store. Regular visits mean you establish a relationship with that store, and sometimes the designer serves you themselves. They can tell the story and inspiration behind a particular piece which connects you with that garment. This whole experience gives a sense of purpose and meaning behind your purchase.

AS CLOSE TO HOME AS POSSIBLE

A positive step we can all take is to buy from as close to home as possible, whether that means down the street or within your own country. The level of impact our purchase has depends on whether everything about the garment was made locally or only some parts of it. When 100% of the garment is produced within the same region, like Australia for example, it would be the ideal. This would mean the natural fabrics you love so much are grown, made and sourced within the country. It would mean each garment is also sewn, constructed, packaged and delivered as close by as possible. While local fabric production is often not possible, we can still aim for this as an ideal.

Most of the time designers are having their collections or a percentage of their garments made overseas. It's likely the fabrics are sourced in Japan, and the buttons, zips and so on from Italy, for example. Then they are shipped to a place like Cambodia to be sewn in less than ideal conditions. All this before being flown to your home country for sale. This is hugely energy intensive, and it puts a strain on the environment. Supporting local designers can also mean we are giving strength to local manufacturing, keeping more money and work in the economy.

Brands who design and make their garments entirely locally are in the minority, however they do set a new standard. There are many benefits when a garment is created this way. It means jobs are given to local workers and there is greater control of labour standards. It also means a smaller footprint on the environment as well as a better level of quality control overall. So, ultimately you end up with a higher quality garment. You are also purchasing a bucket of contentment knowing that people and the environment were taken into consideration while making your beautiful new purchase.

I'm sure you have questions, thinking about this high ideal. It may seem like a pipe dream or a little far off. But imagine as the industry starts to shift and we start producing more and more locally, other people in the supply chain will want to make the change too. Take wool in Australia for example; we produce a high percentage of the world's wool, some of the highest quality in the world, and yet we don't have an industry to process this wool and turn it into yarn. It is nearly all done offshore. Imagine if we could bring this industry back to Australia. That would cut huge amounts of carbon emissions as well as contribute to the economy. But the demand needs to be there, and this means there needs to be a shift in a cultural mindset: the culture of fashionistas. The culture of appreciating local goods, the culture of the industry, and government.

WHAT WILL IT COST?

You may also be wondering how much this is going to cost you. It's true that the cost of clothing will be higher than the prices we have become accustomed to. But isn't that a good thing? If we are going for a more refined wardrobe, with fewer pieces that are better quality, we will have greater satisfaction and they will last longer, provided we choose well. Committing to greater quality saves us money over time.

You may also be questioning whether this limits your ability to find stylish items. Buying locally does require a shift in the way we approach our wardrobes. It may take time to find the right clothing, especially when we have something particular in mind. Overall, if you are looking for basic items there are more brands these days producing quality shirts, pants, dresses, sweaters and the rest in ethical and sustainable ways. Think of it like a new exploration. You will rediscover local brands and experience the joy of finding stunning new options you were unaware of, right in your backyard. It may even plug you into a new sense of community. Having 'local' as part of your ethos will play a big part in making better buying decisions.

Let's also broaden our perspective of local. This can also mean finding vintage items in consignment stores or exchanging items with close friends. Of course, we're not going to exchange an old t-shirt. We can, though, pass on interesting and quality items that will continue to be treasured by someone else.

Beware also of buying local for local's sake. Getting carried away in the moment of a lovely shopping experience on a sunny day doesn't always mean you will love it when you get home. So make sure that it ticks the boxes of your personal style along with as many sustainable points as possible. The most important thing is to make sure it truly suits your aesthetic.

As we bring our focus to locally made garments, we contribute in so many ways, and in time we may find everyone benefits as a result.

CHAPTER 56

The rise of the artisan

'Traditional high-quality craftsmanship is a source of economic opportunity and personal fulfillment.' — Zolaykha Sherzad

As local design becomes more important, we will also turn towards the talent and creativity of the artisans in our community. An artisan is traditionally a person who cultivates their skill and turns it into an art. Sometimes machinery is required, although this especially applies when making things by hand.

When it comes to fashion, some of the most beautiful cultural pieces have been made by artisans who come from a rich heritage. People whose skills have been passed down through many generations. It's the creativity and skill of a handmade item that makes it stand out from the rest. If globalisation and mass production have seen traditional valuable skills like spinning, hand weaving, hand and natural dyeing, and embroidery gradually disappear, now is the time to protect them.

Returning to the handmade is a growing trend, and the more we advance technologically it seems the more there is also a growing interest in the slower aspects of life. This includes garments that are handmade, tailored, embroidered and made as a one-off or part of a small collection. There is so much more love and respect for an item when you invest in it because of the time and effort it took to create.

As we become more considered in the way we consume, the relevance of handmade items will take hold. Each garment will take on new significance and people will want to know the maker and where their item comes from. This means that the stories of our clothes will become more and more important and our values will return to well-made and creative items.

When we talk about protecting traditional crafts and artisan techniques, this can extend from the true definition of the word 'artisan' all the way through to contemporary local makers who are committed to a slow method of production. Perhaps it's an Indigenous artist who weaves beautiful textiles, or a local designer who creates her own patterns and embroiders every garment with unique motifs.

This trend towards the artisan is about protecting old crafts as well as choosing the handmade over mass production. It means keeping traditional skills alive whatever they look like. I feel this will become more and more relevant in the future. That there will be a new appreciation of artisanal fabrics and garments.

VOILA ... MAGIC

In France, Chanel has invested in some of the oldest artisanal companies in the country to preserve their time-honoured skills and take them into the 21st century. One of these companies is Atelier Lognon, one of France's last hand pleaters, which was founded by Gérard Georges Lognon in 1853 and Chanel acquired in 2013. A lot of pleating in the fashion industry is now done by machine, but the work of an artisan pleater can create exceptional shapes and the variations are almost infinite. Lognon has approximately 3000 different moulds or designs in their collection, and some of the moulds which create the pleated fabric date back to 1900.

Using fabric like silk, organza or tulle, it is first ironed flat before placing it between two sheets of pleated card – the mould. The expanse of card is then hand folded and set, before putting it into a type of oven in temperatures reaching 100 degrees for approximately an hour to an hour and a half. After being left to cool for a day, the fabric is then taken out of the mould ... *et voila* ... magic. This kind of handwork may be in the minority these days and be out of budget for many designers, but preserving these types of traditions is so important.

Chanel recognises that the unique and intricate designs they produce rely on the work of specialists like Lognon. In 1997, they established the Paraffection subsidary, translated as 'for love', which now includes some of the oldest artisan houses in France. These artisan houses or ateliers are specialists, like a 140-year-old knitwear specialist, and the incredible embroiderer Lesage which was established in 1924.

Chanel also understands that the heritage of fashion is upheld by these diminishing traditions. These artisans are escorting Chanel into a new age where human creativity and the emotion behind it are valued.

There are highly skilled artisans around the world who specialise in specific and time-honoured crafts. Having garments embroidered in India for example can produce some of the most intricate designs possible, and they are made of impeccable quality. It's time for these artisans to be given the full recognition they deserve. Many brands pay much less to have exquisite work done in developing countries than they do in Europe.

As the world starts to expand its notion of what status and success mean, we can move away from considering luxury from France or Italy to be the only true elegance. What if artisanal pieces from these other dedicated and talented people around the world were just as prized and honoured? My wish is that artisans around the world receive equal and fair reward. In this way we will be able to protect the unique heritage and language of the cultures these people belong to. As we move closer to an appreciation of the handmade and the locally made, it would be great if smaller communities could thrive on the crafts that make them unique.

Personally I have always loved the richness and texture that a cultural piece can bring to my wardrobe. I feel that personal style is enhanced by a truly world view. For example, living in India made me appreciate colour as well as embroidery. I have some pieces that have these elements and I use them to accentuate my wardrobe. I love to think about the small communities who have produced these items. And the story that a single line of colour or embroidery can tell about a culture far different from my own.

To celebrate artisan work and to appreciate the handmade means we don't need to look far outside our own communities. We can find pieces that are made with incredible skill and creativity right on our own doorsteps. To move away from the fast model of fashion means we can put our money behind local designers. Imagine if we could support local production and handmade skills so that they thrive around the world. What a wonderful world that would be.

CHAPTER 57

Radical transparency

'Complete, spontaneous, ego-free transparency.'
— Bruno Pieters

Years ago a friend told me about a new fashion brand that was doing something radical. The high-fashion brand was called Honest By, and it was pushing the boundaries of the industry to become one of the first fully transparent fashion brands.

Led by designer Bruno Pieters, the brand revealed to its customer every detail about how the clothing was made and how much it cost them. Next to each garment on the website was a full-page description and breakdown of where their fabrics and materials came from, how much they cost, who made their clothes, and every single cost along the supply chain. The description showed the true cost of production in relation to the retail price of the garment. It was then up to the customer to decide if it was right for them.

At that time, no one else was doing what Honest By had put into practice. It was when transparency and ethical issues were just starting to trend. It was just as much of a statement to the world about transparency as it was a passion to create well-made garments. In an article written by Leah Borromeo for *The Guardian*, Bruno Pieters said:

I started Honest By because I wanted to be proud of my work. Total transparency is easy. The only reason it doesn't happen is because consumers don't understand that they can demand it. If people asked for it, it can happen tomorrow.

I remember being so impressed at this new approach. It pushed the boundaries and it really resonated with me. It was at a time when I was personally becoming aware of the bigger issues surrounding the industry. I was learning that a cheap t-shirt probably wasn't that cheap after all. Honest By was risking their own profits by being transparent about their pricing. They were challenging the current fashion system by disclosing information about their suppliers. They were also one of the first to talk about who was making their clothes and where they were being made. Promoting change in the industry was more important to them than creating clothes just for the sake of it. They wanted to bring back the value of a garment.

A POWERFUL TOOL FOR CHANGE

So what is radical transparency and why does it matter? Radical transparency is a realignment of the values within a business. It means caring more about the impact it has on the environment and the lives of others than merely running a business to make money. Radical transparency is being honest about all aspects of a business's practices, right through its supply chain. It can also require disclosing how much it takes to make a product alongside the retail price, as was done by Honest By.

Transparency brings awareness that can encourage long-term accountability in the way a fashion business runs. Radical transparency can be a powerful tool for change. After disclosing their practices, fashion brands also need to have very clear targets to keep them on track and constantly evolving.

Moving towards transparency with greener and more ethical ways of producing clothing is a complex issue. It calls for a willingness to adapt within businesses and supply chains. It requires a complete shift of values and actions, whether producing at scale or on a smaller model. There is no quick fix, but at the same time change must happen because the world's resources are diminishing, climate change is escalating, and the inequality that exists within the supply chain must end. We need a radical shift.

We will be the ones to force fashion brands to adapt. Our fashion choices will be guided by a new set of values, choosing brands that tell us where and how our clothes are made. We won't just choose any brand that gives us this information; it will be the ones who have also adjusted their way of doing things. Brands that begin to create clothes that can be recycled easily, that are non-toxic, that are made by people who are paid fairly. We will choose new brands who come on the market over old ones because their whole business is focused on better ways of doing things.

In an ideal world, fashion brands will plan their collections with this in mind, knowing that everything they do and all the processes of sourcing and creating a garment are being held to account. They will be guided by a whole new set of values.

The brands that will survive will be the ones who recognise this is now the only way to do business. It will allow them to collaborate with the industry in new ways and achieve greater and greater sustainability goals. They will also realise that we, their customers, will not engage with them unless they are transparent and accountable for their practices.

Brands will have a dedicated section on their websites telling us their vision for the future. They will share with us the relationships they have with suppliers; for example, we will see the story of a boutique wool farm, and how the wool is lovingly shorn and collected. We'll see the faces of the people who make the clothes and hear about how the money they receive from working contributes to communities and families. These brands will also share the non-toxic processes they use to treat fabrics and garments as they are being created. Transparency will be embedded in the brand DNA.

What will you and I be looking for as we scan a business to find out where it stands? Here is a list that will help to get you started (inspired by the Good on You brand rating system).

People

- Proof that their factories don't demand forced labour.

- Assurance of safe working environments.

- Standards for gender equality.

- Ethical working environments.

- Payment of a living and fair wage.

- Do their factories have unions to protect workers' rights?

Planet

- Disclosing the use of resources — where and how they are sourced.

- Does the brand commit to circular practices?

- Do they address microfibre pollution and aim to eliminate it in their fabrics?

- Disclosure of energy use in the business across transportation, supply chain and business practices.

- What are the carbon emissions created in the business? Are there targets to reduce them?

- What is the business's impact on water?

- Look for disclosure around chemical use in the supply chain and within fabric production.

- How does a brand deal with chemical disposal during production?

Animals

- Does a brand trace the treatment of the animals it sources its fibres from, and what are the practices used?

- Does the brand have animal policies or refuse animal products altogether?

- Is there certified animal welfare in their supply chain?

- Are they committed to eliminating the use of exotic animal hairs, fur, feathers and skins?

- Can a brand trace the farming practices and animal treatment in its supply chain?

Being radical means looking at the process as a whole. As consumers realise the impact of even one garment that is discarded into landfill, we will only pay for clothing that is biodegradable and we will expect that there is a plan for how it is recycled when it wears out. This information won't just be a display to coerce customers, it will be an accepted standard by the fashion industry.

Radical transparency calls on a greater set of values. We can choose brands that are being honest about every part of their business. Brands that care and are committed to a more sustainable fashion future. As I mentioned earlier, like any change, radical transparency starts with *us*. As we look into our wardrobes we will see a collection of pieces that are truly in line with our values.

CHAPTER 58

Responsible production

'Make much less, make it better and make it more expensive.'
— Li Edelkoort

Design can be inspirational; it can also be thoughtful, progressive and visionary. It's through design that our clothing is made both functional as well as beautiful. These days it's more than the aesthetics or beauty of clothing that need to be taken into account if production can truly be considered successful.

The future of fashion lies in a transformational approach. First of all, it demands that businesses produce way less than they have been. This is not an easy task, but there is no alternative. Especially as I write this book and the world is in lockdown due to Covid-19, the fashion industry is reassessing and rethinking the unrealistic pace of production it has been caught up in. In a recent interview with the *Australian Financial Review*, Giorgio Armani said the industry has been 'churning out far too much ill-conceived product that nobody needs'. He said that Covid-19 has 'made me think about what I would like to change in how I approach the fashion system'.

These comments have been reiterated by many other designers during the pandemic. It has forced them to review their business models. This should have happened a long time ago. One of the most success-ful Indian designers — Sandeep Khola of the brand of Khosla Jani — was interviewed in a webinar titled 'Fashion & the Brave New World', where he reflected the same sentiment, saying: 'The way forward for us is that we've been thinking, rethinking, redesigning, looking at things and saying maybe we just have to do the finest and the best for the fewest.'

PIECES WE WILL WANT TO KEEP FOR YEARS TO COME

This new way forward would mean there is more of a focus on quality and design, in pieces that we will want to keep for years to come. So truly responsible production is about reducing quantity and slowing down the pace of the industry. The future of fashion also asks that fashion brands focus on a regenerative and more efficient model, and this is where a circular economy comes into play.

Truly sustainable fashion has never been about a trend or providing an easy solution – it requires a wholistic approach. As I mentioned earlier in the book, a circular fashion economy is one that thinks with the end in mind. According to the UK-based charity WRAP (Waste & Resources Action Programme), up to 80% of a product's environmental impact is determined at the design stage. This means that forward thinking is needed if we are to create garments which have minimal or zero impact on the planet.

A circular economy in fashion takes into account:

- the efficient use of materials

- designing out chemical use

- using renewable resources

- making sure natural systems are regenerated

- implementing regenerative agriculture

- recycling textiles back into raw materials so they can be used again.

Responsible production looks at not just one of these areas but all of them, setting targets to incorporate them in a business over time. This is what Stella McCartney has done in so many ways, and it is visible on her website. You can track her commitments from converting to sustainably sourced viscose right through to investing in farming practices that keep the soil fertile and nourished. This truly is a wholistic perspective because it looks at every single element of a business and how it can reduce its impact on the planet.

On the website of Stella McCartney it states: 'We believe that the future of fashion is circular — it will be restorative and regenerative by design and the clothes we love never end up as waste.' This is a concise description of what I hope many fashion brands will be able to achieve in the near future.

From the outset, as fashion companies take a new approach to design incorporating a responsible method of production, it will push new and innovative design. It can be a refreshing approach to the old, tired wheel of production. Imagine better fabrics, safer work environments with fewer chemicals, and less waste. Doesn't this push creativity to a new level not only for designers but for all areas of business? And isn't design about approaching the new, adapting to the times and looking forward? When the design of the future takes care of the planet as well as producing new and innovative materials and beautiful long-lasting garments, we will be a long way on the road to truly responsible production.

CHAPTER 59

Recycling as a real option

'The simplest way to extend the life of your clothes is by giving them a new owner.' — Patrick Duffy

Discussion of recycling in the fashion industry is almost non-existent — it truly needs a lot more attention. People think that recycling is sending their clothes to charity for it to be resold, however there is so much more than that.

Recycling actually implies the ability to turn our clothing like t-shirts, jeans and dresses back into fibres and remake them into new clothing. Or at the very least, provide an option where once they are turned into fibres they are made into other materials like household and furniture textiles.

The problem is that currently only 1% of textiles are recycled into new garments. As we have heard many times throughout this book, textile waste is a huge issue, with vast amounts of polyester clothing ending up in landfill or being incinerated. With recycling we want to divert more clothing from landfill and keep it in use through true recycling, just as plastic bottles are recycled and turned into fabrics, or more plastic bottles.

This truly is a huge and difficult issue, because when our garments are made, many times they are composed of more than one fibre. For example, when you look at your woollen sweater and it says 40% wool and 50% polyester, it's not so easy to separate the wool from the polyester.

I recently came across an article by AG CHEMI GROUP which spoke about the challenges of textile recycling. This article quoted Hanna de la Motte, a textile recycling chemist. She said:

> You cannot take a well-used cotton t-shirt, mechanically tear it apart and then make the cotton fibres into a new cotton t-shirt, because they have lost so much fibre quality that the t-shirt will not be of high enough quality to fit into the market.

So, as you can see, textile recycling faces many hurdles, and is really at the beginning of its cycle of adoption and innovation. There are currently no accessible options for people like you and me who simply want to find a place to take our clothing that has holes and stains so that it can be recycled into new fibres. This puts the impetus back on us to be considered about what we buy. There are some fashion brands who are looking at ways to take back their clothing once it has come to the end of its life, but the people who are doing it are in the minority and it's in its infancy. There are some brands like Eileen Fisher in USA who have a take back system called RENEW which allows you to bring your clothes back beyond your closet. They will find returned clothes a new home or turn them into entirely new designs. Eileen Fisher's clothes are more easily able to be recycled than others because they are sourced from organic or quality sustainable fibres and are free of the harmful dyes.

In 2018, $3 million of Eileen's $500 million in revenue came from this RENEW project which shows that people like you and I really want to be part of the movement for change. Eileen Fisher uses a high-tech felting machine which repurposes returned fabrics and turns them into stylish accessories, wall fixtures and pieces of art. This type of recycling allows the Eileen Fisher brand to be truly circular in its approach.

So what can we do? We can put pressure on our governments to put their focus on textile recycling. It will save a lot of resources, divert textiles from landfill, and keep these textiles in the loop, creating new economic possibilities.

AVOIDING CLOTHING AND TEXTILE WASTE IS THE BEST ACTION YOU CAN TAKE

Aside from this, avoiding clothing and textile waste is the best action you can take. I have come up with a list for you to keep your focus on making the best decisions possible when it comes to your clothing. You can do this through:

- buying less clothing

- buying better clothing, keeping it in use longer and avoiding throwing it out

- taking care of what you have

- being aware of the textile composition, buying product that is as pure and high quality as possible

- buying recycled fabrics such as recycled polyester

- avoiding fast fashion that will be unusable in a short amount of time

- adopting the reuse and relove strategies I mentioned earlier.

Overall, we need to elevate our consciousness and approach to fashion if we want to avoid textile waste. This means thinking about the use of a garment before buying it and asking yourself if it is actually functional for your lifestyle.

Make a commitment that you will only buy clothing you will wear for a long time. It must be high quality, durable and well designed, so that you are extremely happy with it. It should be beautiful and pleasing to your overall sense of style and fashion. You must love your clothing and be committed to taking care of it and keeping it forever. This is the best we can do, and hopefully in the future there will be many truly incredible energy-efficient and environmentally friendly options for textile recycling.

CHAPTER 60

Taking care of people

'People, even more than things, have to be restored, renewed, revived, reclaimed, and redeemed.' — Audrey Hepburn

Setting our sights on a truly transformed fashion industry is only complete when we consider the people who work every day to produce our clothing and the materials they are made from. When we consider that these people have needs, wants and desires just like you and me, it becomes a question of ethics. Now that we have knowledge about what goes on, we must act and make choices that contribute to ethical and supportive conditions within fashion supply chains.

When I think about the big corporations who blatantly choose profit over the dignity of their workers' lives, and in many cases have no awareness of the conditions in the factories where their clothes are created, I am reminded there is no easy answer. There are just so many issues involved.

THE REVOLUTION HAS BEGUN

Fortunately there are organisations and movements like Fashion Revolution that are working for policy change and reform across the board. They are working for systemic change and showing us how we can get involved. But what can you and I do today? It all comes back to asking better questions and doing better research. We need to be making informed decisions.

Where do we begin? We start with the brands that we normally shop from, the ones we adore. Firstly, we find out if they are publicising information about who makes their clothes. Are they taking care of the people in their supply chain? Do they have approved independent auditing of the factories they use? If they aren't obviously telling us, we can get involved; send them an email and ask questions to find out. If you fail to get an answer, then can we still buy from them? It's up to us to make the call. It really is a re-evaluation of our values and the kind of world we would like to see.

It is a lot easier to manage and keep an eye on fair work standards when factories are small or brands are working with local communities for production. But when it gets to bigger brands and bigger factories, even with auditing it is much harder to be sure of ethical standards. I believe the answer comes back to artisanal and local production. In this way it's more likely our clothing is not only made with passion and attention to detail, there is more likelihood of it being better quality and worthy to be kept for a lifetime.

When I worked in France for a fashion brand, they were able to keep an eye on their production; some was done in house, some in regional areas, and other work in small factories in neighbouring European countries which they visited regularly. At that time there wasn't as much demand for brands to be transparent, so they weren't putting it on their website or social media, however being a smaller brand they had much more control.

It's up to us to search for this information before we buy. Hopefully when enough people stand up and say they want full disclosure and fair work practices, brands will take notice. It's a bit like blood diamonds. Before people knew about what went on, these diamonds were sought after and extremely valuable. But once the word was out and people learnt that not all diamonds are equal and that children were being forced into labour and people were killed to mine these diamonds, people united. The diamonds lost their value. It was people who brought the awareness — it was a movement that created the change.

There are smaller brands in Melbourne (where I live) who are committed to keeping their production in house, and I'm sure you have designers in your city or country who are also able to keep an eye on their production and how the people who make their clothes are taken care of.

I recently went online to look at a couple of smaller Melbourne brands who are committed to a new and fairer world of fashion. One brand, Arnsdorf, states on their website:

> We've taken almost everything in-house, from design to production, so we can ensure we can get products to you that are always of exceptional quality, ethically sound and always transparent. And we're committed to transparency, that's why when you browse our products, you can always know where they were made, the people who made them and at what cost.

When you go to a product on their website you can click on a tab that says 'Who made this product?' and it will tell you the exact names of the people involved. And there are more and more brands doing the same.

I see this as the future of fashion. We need to be able to rely on the brands we invest in doing the right thing. I'm so hopeful when I see transparency like this that the movement is going to grow. We can see, from the big brands to the small independent designers, that this is becoming the new standard, the new normal. Get on board so we can push for change with our questions and actions. We know what we must do; let's make an ethical decision and place the value of our clothing with the people, hands and hearts who make them.

CHAPTER 61

Fabric technology and innovation

'I hope technology will save us and create a newness to an industry that really needs it. Why are we the only people not working so closely with technology and yet we're supposed to be at the forefront of everything? We're in danger of being left behind.' — Stella McCartney

The fabric that our clothing is made of needs to be pleasing to touch and beautiful in its appearance before we want to wear it. The days of ugly hemp clothing are behind us because fibres like this have now been innovated so that they are elegant and refined as a fabric. Sustainable textiles have truly taken a huge leap forward and are advancing rapidly.

THE NEW WAY FORWARD

The future of our clothing relies on the innovation of the way fabric and textiles are created. This is where the convergence of technology and fashion is truly the new way forward. It means finding new methods of sourcing raw materials and turning them into fabrics with minimal impact on the environment. It also depends on a more energy-efficient process to produce them. Finally, it involves a whole new type of thinking to create fabrics that are environmentally friendly and made out of materials we haven't thought of yet. Some of this is already happening.

Predominantly I recommend natural fibres over synthetic ones, and when building a sustainable wardrobe, you — like me — might decide to steer clear of any fabrics that come from manmade fibres like recycled plastic, just another type of polyester that carries chemicals with it. I do feel, however, that I need to make you aware of some of these recycled fabrics, because they are doing a lot to reduce the impact of plastic waste. They are also regenerative and restorative by design rather than extracting new raw materials from the environment.

Recycling plastic into fabric is a big part of fashion these days, but not all of these fabrics are created equal. Make sure the plastic used is being taken from post-consumer plastic — such as plastic bottles that have been discarded as waste — and not pre-consumer plastic which is basically offcuts of the industry that hasn't been used yet.

Many fashion brands are starting to make their clothing out of fabrics that are made of recycled plastic bottles. As we know, at least 60% of textiles are made of polyester which comes from petroleum, which is hugely damaging on the environment. Rather than continually creating more polyester we can at least use the huge amounts of plastic already created. This diverts plastic from landfill and puts it to good use. You would be surprised to touch these fabrics; they can be super soft and feel lovely to touch. You would not even think that they were made from such materials.

Another type of fabric being produced is from recycled fishing nets. Yes, fishing nets — they are clogging up our oceans and killing marine life, but fashion is putting them to good use with a fabric called ECONYL®, which is regenerated nylon. It is created by an Italian firm called Aquafil. ECONYL® is a type of nylon yarn made up of industrial waste, fishing nets and fabric waste. The process used to create ECONYL® is regenerative and efficient. It uses less water and creates less waste than traditional methods. It regenerates old product and turns it into the new. Again, the final fabrics are soft to touch and pleasurable to wear.

Fabric innovation also relies on rethinking the way we source fibres so that they are damaging the environment as little as possible. This means rather than cutting down ancient forests to create wood pulp which is turned into viscose, making sure it is taken from sustainable sources. This means using forests in a way that maintains nature's biodiversity. It means sourcing wood in a way that makes sure nature's ability to produce and regenerate is nurtured.

This means farming also needs to be included when we talk about textile innovation. Large-scale farming is responsible for much of the depletion of our land. Farming includes the production of cotton, wool and other fibres. Farming destroys the biodiversity of nature, depleting natural ecosystems that are key to the planet's survival. This is where regenerative agriculture comes into play. It is a long-term solution that takes time to turn things around. It is future-focused and requires a commitment now to make sure the earth can replenish itself.

Regenerative agriculture is about giving back to the earth all the goodness we take from it. According to the non-profit organisation Regeneration International: 'Regenerative Agriculture describes farming and grazing practices that, among other benefits, reverse climate change by rebuilding soil organic matter and restoring degraded soil biodiversity.' Considering that much of our clothing requires the use of agriculture, protecting the earth's biodiversity is key to the future of fabric and textile innovation.

A NEW TEXTILES FUTURE

There are other types of fabric innovation taking place around the world. Individuals and start ups are dedicating their time to pushing the boundaries; some are in the developmental stage but all efforts are working towards a new textiles future. These textiles represent new areas of previously unused resources. Some are already in production. They create fully biodegradable and beautiful fabrics. Included in these fabrics are bio yarn made of kelp fibres, fabrics made of banana fibres and lotus fibres, and fabrics made of coffee grounds. There are also silks made from crop waste, pineapple fabric, vegan leather that comes from grape waste, and fabric made from algae and mushrooms. The list goes on, and as you can see there is some incredible scope out there. And over time these new fabrics truly will be a part of our lives.

Technology is also being used to bypass the waste created by the fashion industry altogether. There has been a lot of research and growth in start ups looking to use technology to create custom-made garments to order. In the traditional model of fashion clothing is made in bulk, and many times a brand only sells a portion of its collection, leaving a lot of money and resources on the table.

There is a brand called Citizen Wolf in Australia who is utilising technology, algorithms and big data to produce custom made t-shirts only when they are ordered. In the words of Citizen Wolf founder Zoltan Czaski:

> Our business is built on on-demand manufacturing. We only make it if we've sold it. So we don't sit on stock, we don't go on sale, we're not seasonal, we're not trend-led. That means that we can run a much leaner business, and a much more sustainable one.

The future of our clothing has never been more exciting. With the regeneration of old materials and the advancement of the new, I have a lot of hope for the future of fashion. We can look forward to many new and beautiful textiles in the future. Keep your minds, eyes and ears open so you will be able to spot them when you come across them on your next shopping trip.

CHAPTER 62

And finally, what will our wardrobes look like?

'The least possible impact but it still has beauty, desirability and is well designed.' — Gabriela Hearst

Our wardrobes of the future will be a more refined version of their former selves. As we become more considered, we will be able to look inside and see a truly well curated selection of garments. Any new pieces we purchase will be a conscious addition of something that has longevity, is beautiful, has been sourced with care, and has a purpose.

So what do we see when we open up those doors? Let's take a look. The first and most obvious change is that we will have fewer clothes overall. We will have fallen in love with our existing wardrobes in new ways through seeing them with different eyes. Because of the desire to create a truly sustainable wardrobe, we will discover how to wear our clothing in new combinations and styles. This is key; loving everything that we own and keeping it in use as long as possible.

Another unexpected benefit of rediscovering our wardrobes will be giving new life to pieces we didn't wear because they were damaged or out of date. Having made friends with an alterations specialist, we will create updated shapes and styles and these pieces will find their place in our wardrobes once again. They will be on a high rotation among regularly worn outfits because of this new appreciation.

Our fewer clothes will be better quality. We will have sorted out the pieces of lesser quality and found new homes or new purposes for them. Each piece that remains will have a specific appeal. Whether it's the new pieces or old, they will be items that retain their wearability over many years. Each will be durable and beautiful because of the way it was designed. There is nothing like a wardrobe full of well-made clothes that each have a unique wow factor.

Our clothes will each have a specific story to tell, and we'll feel good about them because they are sustainable. We'll know the history of each item, its production, where it came from, and the fields that produced them, almost like the genetics of clothing – each part of their DNA will be known to us.

It's these stories that will give us the most enjoyment. Whether it's a handwoven woollen jacket with a unique texture or an organic cotton shirt dress that was dyed with a sustainably produced natural dye. It's these pieces that will have been made with care and deliberate attention. We will know the stories of the people who made our clothing, and be proud to tell others about the way their lives are thriving as they produce their art. These pieces will feel, look and speak of quality and elegance.

The fabrics will be soft to touch, chemical free, and made of high-quality natural fibres. They will breathe with our body and speak of simple, understated luxury. We will have less and less polyester or fabrics made of plastic. If they are made of polyester they will be from brands committed to fabrics that have been recycled and sourced sustainably.

Taking a closer look at the intricacies of our personal collections, they will be interspersed with different fabrics, textures and colours. We will have carefully found vintage pieces that fit our style and elevate our look to a new level. We will have cultural pieces and those made by artisans. The artisanal garments will show skill, personality and a love of culture.

Our intentionally crafted wardrobes will be a homage to stories of our lives, our families, and everything we hold dear. We will be at ease and confident knowing our sense of self is fully expressed in the beautiful pieces we own. They will be a more refined, elegant and authentic version of who we are and they will demonstrate the highest regard we hold for ourselves, the people who make our clothes and nature.

CHAPTER 63

Where to from here?

Thank you for taking the time to read this far. We've covered a lot of ground. I truly appreciate you picking up this book and investing your time to rethink your relationship with fashion. In doing so you are also considering the positive impact our fashion choices have on the lives of others and the future of the planet.

Thank you for letting me share my knowledge, thoughts and experience with you, as well as some of the things I've found that can pave the way to a new world of fashion. I hope this book gives you the tools to design a wardrobe that you truly love. I hope it has helped you to establish a greater sense of self-respect and inspired you to commit to honouring yourself in every way.

When we truly value ourselves, we show this to others naturally. It makes us want to take care of others and live in a way that respects the world around us. It's my hope that rethinking your fashion has opened up a greater world view and inspired you to live a life of true wellbeing.

Let's make a decision to choose our fashion in alignment with an elevated set of values that empower others and are beneficial for the environment. Don't underestimate for a second the influence you can have as an individual.

WORKING WITH LALITA

If you've enjoyed *It's Time to Rethink Your Fashion* and you'd like to find out more about working with Lalita Lowe there are a number of options on the following pages.

Personal Fashion Curation Service

Would you like to work with Lalita to develop your very own stylish collection of clothes that represent the values in this book? Would you like to feel attractive and confident in the clothes you wear while also doing good morally and environmentally? Work with Lalita to build a sustainable wardrobe of beautiful clothes that meet your budget, lifestyle and aesthetic needs.

The way Lalita works with her clients is unique and individual to each person. It can involve reworking your existing wardrobe, shopping for new pieces or a combination of both. Lalita usually starts with a customised fashion strategy to determine your needs and goals. From there a clear plan of action is created and the curation of your own amazing collection of lifetime pieces begins. To find out more visit www.lalitalowe.com.

Rethink Your Fashion Course

Do you want to know how to build a truly wonderful collection of clothes that is not only beautiful but sustainable as well? One that has been purchased out of respect for the people who created your clothes as well as the wellbeing of the planet?

In this course you will be taken step by step through Lalita's process for choosing clothing consciously and ensuring your wardrobe is filled with the perfect pieces. Remember, just because it's sustainable doesn't mean it can't be beautiful.

This course will help you:

- create your own fashion manifesto

- learn about the three key elements when choosing a new garment: fit, fabric and construction

- learn how to decode brands and what they stand for

- choose fabrics that will last and maintain their quality over years

- learn how to keep your clothes in perfect condition for as long as possible

- create an annual budget for your clothing

- ... and so much more.

To find out more visit: www.lalitalowe.com.

The Curatorial (www.curatorial.global)

Coming soon, your very own online curated collection of vintage pieces to choose from. Sourced by Lalita, her keen eye for detail, quality, colour and artisanship will create a unique selection of pre-loved pieces. These will be available for you to find your next wardrobe staple or statement piece. You can register your interest to be notified of the launch at: www.curatorial.global.

Speaking

Have Lalita speak at your next event (live or virtual).

One thing that Lalita loves to talk about is helping people to rethink their relationship to fashion. She can do this through live and virtual events such as conferences, workshops, online summits and training seminars. And some of the specific top topics that Lalita can cover are:

- rethinking our values and relationship to fashion

- the current state of the fashion industry

- why the industry is being called to evolve

- what we can do as active consumers

- the future of fashion

If you'd like to find out more about getting Lalita to speak at your event, please get in touch with her via the website: www.lalitalowe.com.

Media Interviews

If you'd like to interview Lalita for any form of media, including podcast shows about the concept of this book, specifically the topic of rethinking our fashion collectively and individually, then please contact Lalita and her team at info@lalitalowe.com.